Essentials of
Collection Law

Steven M. Bragg

AccountingTools®

ISBN 978-1-64221-139-9

For more information about AccountingTools® products, visit our Web site at www.accountingtools.com.

Table of Contents

About the Author

Steven Bragg, CPA, has been the chief financial officer or controller of four companies, as well as a consulting manager at Ernst & Young. He received a master's degree in finance from Bentley College, an MBA from Babson College, and a Bachelor's degree in Economics from the University of Maine. He has been a two-time president of the Colorado Mountain Club, and is an avid alpine skier, mountain biker, and certified master diver. Mr. Bragg resides in Centennial, Colorado. He has written more than 300 books and courses, including *New Controller Guidebook*, *GAAP Guidebook*, and *Payroll Management*. He has also written the science fiction novel *Under an Autumn Sun*, first book in *The Auditors* trilogy.

Steven maintains the accountingtools.com web site, which contains continuing professional education courses, the Accounting Best Practices podcast, and thousands of articles on accounting subjects.

Chapter 1
Sales Contracts

Introduction

When dealing with collection law, we must start with the concept of the sales contract, in order to have a clear understanding of the rights and obligations of the buyer and seller. The key laws governing sales contracts are contained within Article 2 of the Uniform Commercial Code (UCC). The topics addressed include contract formation, contract acceptance, who bears the risk of loss, and the remedies available to the seller and buyer when a contract is breached – along with several related topics. We cover these issues in the following pages, along with supporting examples.

Essential Terminology

Several terms are routinely employed when discussing sales contracts. One is a *sale*, which is the transfer of goods from a seller to a buyer for a price. For example, a sale has occurred when an electric bicycle is purchased from a seller for $2,500, irrespective of the form of consideration used. Under the UCC, it is possible for a sales contract to be modified without a change in the associated consideration.

Another key term is *goods*, which are comprised of tangible items that can be transported when they are linked to a contract. For example, a washing machine is defined as goods, since it is both tangible and moveable, while real estate is not considered to be goods, since it cannot be transported.

Article 2 of the UCC does not apply to the sale of services (such as landscaping services and medical services). However, there may be elements of both goods and services in a sale, such as in the remodeling of a room, which predominantly involves labor, but which also includes the installation of drywall. These dual-element sales are known as *mixed sales*. Article 2 applies to mixed sales only when the goods portion of a sale is the predominant element.

The UCC generally applies to any party, whether or not they are classified as a merchant. Some UCC provisions, however, only apply to a merchant. A *merchant* is defined as a party that routinely deals in goods of the kind associated with a transaction, or who holds himself out as having the knowledge or skill associated with such goods. For example, a seller of power tools is considered a merchant with respect to the sale of power tools, but not with respect to the sale of garden supplies.

Contract Formation

A sales contract is formed when there has been a formal offer and acceptance. Offer and acceptance can be construed to have taken place when both parties exhibit behavior indicating that they have entered into such an arrangement. This is the case even when it is not possible to determine the exact moment when the contract was formed.

A contract is not considered to be present just because some essential terms remain undefined, as long as the parties to it intended to form a contract and it is reasonably possible to derive an appropriate remedy. For example, a contract to buy corn from a farmer will be considered valid if its terms merely state that the price will be based on the prices published by the Chicago Mercantile Exchange. If this price is not available as of the sale date, then a court could set a reasonable price that is based on prices available on adjacent days.

In cases where payment terms are not stated in a contract, the UCC holds that payment should occur when the buyer receives the goods – essentially, cash on delivery terms. However, if there is a transfer of title as part of a sale, then payment should occur when the title transfer occurs, even though the physical transfer of goods may occur on some other date.

A contract may not specify where the transfer of goods is to occur. When this is the case, the UCC mandates that the default place of delivery will be the seller's location. If the seller does not have a business location, then the default location is the seller's home address. However, if both parties know that the goods being sold are at an alternative location, then this location becomes the place at which the transfer of goods is to take place.

It is also possible that the delivery period is not specified in a contract. If so, the UCC states that the contract must be performed within a reasonable period of time (which is not defined further).

The Firm Offer Rule

An offeror can rescind an offer at any time prior to its acceptance by the offeree. There is one case in which this is not true, which is called the *firm offer rule*. Under this rule, when a merchant issues a written and signed promise to keep an offer open, this creates an irrevocable offer. The firm offer will only last for the period of time stated in the offer. If no time period for the offer to remain open is stated, then it will stay open for a maximum of three months.

EXAMPLE

Unique Wheels offers to sell an antique Indian motorcycle to Mr. Jones on September 1 for $40,000. This offer includes a written assurance that the offer will remain open until September 15. On September 10, the company sells the motorcycle to another customer. On September 12, Mr. Jones arrives with $40,000 in cash to pay for the motorcycle. Unique Wheels is liable to Mr. Jones for breach of contract. Therefore, if Mr. Jones subsequently buys an Indian motorcycle in the same condition and age from another dealer for $45,000, he can recover the $5,000 difference from Unique Wheels.

Contract Acceptance

When an offer is made for the sale or lease of goods, it can be accepted via any reasonable medium of acceptance.

EXAMPLE

A seller sends an offer to sell goods to a buyer with a text message. The buyer, who is a noted Egyptologist, chisels his acceptance into a block of granite and has it delivered by cart to the seller. This is a valid form of acceptance, though a decidedly odd one.

In cases where an offer to buy goods requires rapid delivery, the buyer's offer is construed as being accepted when the seller promptly ships the goods. In essence, the shipment signals acceptance of the offer.

Contract acceptance occurs only after the receiving party has a reasonable chance to inspect the goods and signifies any one of the following:

- That the goods conform to the receiver's expectations;
- That the goods do not conform to the receiver's expectations, but the receiver will accept them anyways; or
- That the receiver has not rejected the goods after a reasonable period of time.

The acceptance differs markedly when goods are being offered to a buyer as an accommodation. In this case, the goods being sent differ in some respect from what the buyer ordered, so the buyer has the option to reject them.

EXAMPLE

A vermin control business orders a case of wasp spray from a local distributor. The distributor is out of wasp spray and does not expect to be back in stock for at least another month. As an accommodation, the distributor sends a case of aphid spray to the vermin control company instead. Since this is a counteroffer, the buyer has the option to reject the shipment.

A common problem that occurs in commercial sales contracts is that an offer is made using the seller's standard boilerplate terms, while the acceptance from the buyer is made using the buyer's standard boilerplate terms. The result is a conflicting set of contract terms. When this happens, the additional terms included in the buyer's acceptance notification are assumed to be included in the sales contract. One exception to this rule is when the offer made by the seller specifically states that the buyer must accept the terms of the offer. Another exception is when the seller notifies the buyer that these additional terms are not acceptable. When there are material differences between the terms being sent back and forth, a court may declare that there is no contract.

Written Contract Requirements

Contracts for the sale of goods must be in writing when the price exceeds $500.

EXAMPLE

A merchant verbally agrees to sell a used off-terrain vehicle to a buyer for $600. When the buyer shows up the next day with the money, the merchant refuses to sell him the vehicle. The merchant's justification is that the arrangement must be in writing in order to be enforceable, since the $600 price exceeds the $500 threshold level set by the UCC, above which contracts must be in writing.

However, there are cases in which a contract *is* enforceable, even when no written contract is present. One situation arises when a buyer has ordered customized goods. Such a contract is enforceable when the goods are not suitable for sale to other parties, due to their customized nature. A contract is also enforceable when the seller admits that a contract for sale was made between the parties. A third situation in which a verbal contract can be enforced is when one of the parties to an agreement sends a written confirmation of the sale to the other party, and the other party does not issue a written objection within 10 days of receipt of the confirmation; this is known as the written confirmation rule.

EXAMPLE

A merchant in Casper, Wyoming calls a slaughterhouse in Iowa with an offer to sell it 10 head of cattle for $12,000. The next day, the Casper merchant sends an email to the slaughterhouse representative, confirming the terms of the sale. The buyer, who received the email, does not object to the email in writing within 10 days of receipt of the message. This means that the slaughterhouse cannot validly claim that the contract cannot be enforced on the grounds that it was not a written contract.

Parol Evidence Rule

The parol evidence rule governs the extent to which the parties to a case can introduce into court any evidence of a prior or contemporaneous agreement in order to modify a contract. This rule excludes the admission of parol evidence, which means that when the parties to a contract have signed a written contract, any evidence of prior negotiations (known as parol evidence) is not admissible for the purpose of altering what has been written into a contract.

However, there are cases in which the terms of a contract are not clear. When this is the case, it is allowable to refer to sources outside the contract in order to more clearly define these terms. When the information in these sources is not consistent across documents, they are relied upon in the following descending order of priority:

1. The conduct of the parties as it relates to the contract.
2. The conduct of the parties in prior transactions.
3. The manner in which the issue is commonly dealt with within the industry.

EXAMPLE

A merchant that sells various types of pipe enters into a contract with a frequent buyer that stipulates the sale of 300 feet of 1" inside diameter pipe. The material used to construct the pipe is not specified. The merchant ships 300 feet of copper pipe to the buyer, who rejects it.

In the subsequent court proceedings, the court reviews the nature of previous transactions between the two parties, and finds that every shipment made was of copper pipe. The court concludes that the delivery of copper pipe could be assumed, and includes this specification in the contract.

Title to Goods

When the transfer of title to goods occurs will depend on the circumstances, as described in the following sub-sections.

Identification of Goods

The title to goods does not pass to the buyer until they have been identified in a contract. There are several ways in which goods can be identified within a contract. For example, a truck is identified by stating its vehicle identification number. Or, when goods are being ordered in bulk (such as the delivery of 100 bushels of zucchini), then the goods are identified when they have been separated from inventory and tagged as being deliverable to the specific buyer.

Passage of Title

The title to goods can pass from the seller to the buyer using any procedures that the parties agree upon. If no procedure for the passing of title is stated within a contract, then the UCC mandates that title must pass when the seller's performance relating to the delivery of goods is complete.

Shipment Scenarios

When the parties enter into a *shipment contract*, the seller is required to deliver the goods to a common carrier, which then transports them to the buyer. Under this arrangement, title passes at the point of shipment. Alternatively, when the parties enter into a *destination contract*, the seller delivers the goods to the destination specified in the contract, after which title passes to the buyer. When there is no indication in a contract about whether it is a shipment contract or a destination contract, the presumption is that it is a shipment contract.

A third variation arises when the goods are located at a public warehouse, and will remain there; in this situation, title passes when the seller delivers a warehouse receipt to the buyer, so that the buyer now owns the goods. A final scenario is when there is no document of title to be transferred, and the goods are clearly identified when the contract is signed; in this case, title passes when the contract is signed.

EXAMPLE

Mary buys one ton of decorative stones from Landscape Supply for $400. The contract states that she will pick up the stones from Landscape Supply's storage area. Title to the stones passes when both parties sign the contract, even though Mary may not pick up the stones for several weeks.

Remedies for Breach of Sales Contracts

When either party to a sales contract breaches its terms, there are a variety of remedies available to the injured party. The intent behind these remedies is to place the injured party in an equivalent position to what would have been the case if the contract had been properly fulfilled.

Seller Remedies

The basic obligation of the seller in a sales contract is to transfer the required goods to the buyer at the mandated time and place specified in the contract. If the seller finds that the buyer is improperly rejecting goods or not paying in a timely manner, then it has the right to withhold further deliveries of goods. This remedy can extend to halting the delivery of goods that are currently in transit.

A seller can demand the return of goods that have already been delivered to a buyer, though only in two situations. One is when the buyer is paying under credit terms, and the seller learns that the buyer was insolvent; in this case, the seller has 10 days in which to issue a demand for return of the goods. A demand for reclamation can occur at any time (that is, without the 10-day restriction) when the buyer's payment check bounces or when the buyer misrepresents its solvency in writing to the seller within three months of the delivery of goods.

A buyer may repudiate or breach a contract before the seller delivers goods to it. If so, the seller can resell the goods and has the right to recover damages from the buyer. These damages are capped at the difference between the original contract price and the disposition price. If the seller is able to resell the goods at a higher price, the extra profit generated is not payable to the original buyer. The seller also has the right to pursue the buyer for incidental damages associated with the transaction, such as sales commissions, transportation charges, and storage fees.

A buyer's repudiation or breach of a contract may occur before the seller has finished constructing the goods. When this happens, the seller can either scrap the goods, sell them off as-is, or complete the work and sell them elsewhere. In all three cases, the seller can recover damages from the buyer.

> **Note:** When a seller pursues a buyer for damages, the maximum amount that can be awarded is the difference between the market price and contract price of the goods on the date when the goods were delivered, as well as incidental damages. If this damage calculation results in profits lower than would have been the case if full contract performance had occurred, then the seller can also pursue the buyer for lost profits.

Buyer Remedies

If delivered goods do not conform to the requirements of a contract, then the buyer can elect to reject the entire shipment, reject a portion of it, or accept the entire shipment. If the buyer elects to accept the goods, it is still possible to seek other remedies against the seller.

EXAMPLE

A sales contract between a food cart manufacturer and a major theme park stipulates the gauge of steel that shall be used in the carts. The manufacturer then constructs carts using steel that is thinner than what was stipulated in the contract. When all 20 food carts ordered by the theme park are delivered, the park's receiving department discovers that the carts do not conform to the contract specifications. The theme park needs the carts for a grand opening of a new segment of the park in a few days, so it elects to accept the delivery, but then pursues remedies from the manufacturer to have the carts rebuilt to the correct specifications.

When a seller delivers nonconforming goods to the buyer, the seller has an opportunity to repair or replace the goods. This right is available to the seller through the remainder of the performance period specified in the underlying contract, as long as the seller notifies the buyer of its intention to correct the situation.

EXAMPLE

A contract states that the seller will deliver 500 pairs of white running shoes to a shoe retailer by June 30. Instead, the seller delivers 500 pairs of blue running shoes. The retailer rejects the delivery on June 20. The seller has until June 30 to replace the shoes with white ones, as long as it notifies the retailer of its intent to replace the shoes.

A buyer may make an advance payment to a seller for the future delivery of goods, after which the seller becomes insolvent. In this case, the buyer can recover the goods from the seller – as long as the seller becomes insolvent within 10 days of receiving the payment. In order to recover the goods, the buyer must pay any remaining amounts due to the seller under the terms of the underlying contract.

A buyer may have contracted to acquire a unique item, such as a sculpture. In this case, the buyer has the right to obtain specific performance – which means delivery of the unique item. A court can issue a decree of specific performance, which requires the seller to deliver the item to the buyer.

EXAMPLE

A seller offers to sell a unique, one-of-a-kind Monique Ponto watch to a collector for $500,000. The parties draw up and sign a contract to do so, after which the seller refuses to deliver the watch. The collector can sue for specific performance, requiring the seller to deliver the watch.

A variation on the last concept is when a seller is withholding goods, and the buyer is unable to acquire substitute goods elsewhere. In this case, where the goods are not unique but are scarce, a court can order the seller to deliver the specified goods to the buyer.

When a seller does not deliver goods as promised, the buyer can purchase substitute goods, and then recover the difference between the cost of the original goods and the cost of the replacement goods, as well as incidental expenses.

EXPENSES

Albright Energy enters into a contract to buy 500 transformers from International Electric for $1,000 each. The seller breaches the contract and does not deliver the transformers. Albright is forced to acquire the transformers from a backup supplier for $1,200 each. Albright can recover $100,000 (calculated as 500 units × $200 price differential) from International Electric because of its breach of contract.

If a seller fails to deliver goods or repudiates the underlying contract, then the buyer can cancel the contract entirely. This option is also available when the buyer rejects delivered goods for cause. When a contract is cancelled, the buyer is discharged from having any further obligations under the terms of the contract.

Destruction of Goods

Goods are sometimes destroyed in transit, before the risk of loss passes to the buyer. When this happens, the contract is considered to be void, and both parties to the contract are then excused from further contractual performance.

EXAMPLE

A buyer contracts to acquire the latest full-featured toilet from the world-leading Japanese provider of toilets, featuring bacteria-neutralizing ultraviolet light and a titanium dioxide-fired toilet bowl. The buyer contracts to have this modern marvel delivered by air freight. Unfortunately, the plane goes down over the Pacific Ocean with all toilets lost. This product loss voids the contract, and the buyer does not have to pay for the toilet – though he may mourn its loss.

A variation on the concept arises when the goods are only damaged in transit. In this case, the buyer can elect to treat the contract as void, or accept the goods and reduce the purchase price to compensate for the level of damage incurred.

Buyer Acceptance

Once a seller has delivered goods to the buyer, the buyer has the right to inspect them prior to acceptance. If the goods do not conform to the specifications stated in the underlying contract, then the buyer has the right to reject the goods and not pay for them. If there is no provision in the contract for where and when this inspection is to take place, then it should occur at a reasonable time and place. If the goods conform to the contractual requirements, then the buyer pays for the inspection; however, if the goods are rejected due to nonconformance, then the buyer has the right to collect the inspection cost from the seller.

The buyer's acceptance of delivered goods is assumed to have taken place when it has signified that the goods are in conformance, or fails to reject the goods within a reasonable time following the delivery date. If the buyer subsequently resells the goods, then buyer acceptance is assumed to have occurred.

It is possible for a buyer to revoke a prior acceptance of delivered goods. This revocation is legally permissible when the following conditions are present:

- The goods are nonconforming;
- The discovered nonconformity significantly impairs the value of the goods; and
- One of the following issues is present:
  - The seller has not corrected the nonconformity
  - The goods were accepted before the nonconformity was found and the issue was difficult to discover
  - The goods were accepted before the nonconformity was found and the seller issued assurances that the goods were in conformance

Any revocation of an acceptance is not valid until the buyer notifies the seller of it. Further, the revocation must be made within a reasonable time after the nonconformance issue is found. And finally, the revocation must be made before the condition of the goods has changed to a substantial extent.

Assurance of Performance

Both parties to a sales contract are working under the assumption that the other party is performing in accordance with the contract terms. If either party has reasonable grounds to suspect that the other party will not be able to perform, it can demand an adequate assurance of performance in writing. Until it receives such assurance, the party making the demand can suspend its contractual activities.

EXAMPLE

A buyer contracts to purchase several air conditioning units from a well-known local manufacturer, with delivery scheduled for May 1. On April 15, the buyer learns that a water main ruptured next to the manufacturer's facility, flooding it. The buyer immediately issues a demand for adequate assurance of performance, which the manufacturer is not able to provide. Accordingly, the buyer treats the contract as having been repudiated.

Summary

There are many legal issues associated with sales contracts. Issues that frequently arise are whether a contract has been formed, who has title to the goods, when does ownership of the goods pass from the seller to the buyer, and what remedies are available to the parties when a contract is breached. This chapter noted the key decision points upon which these legal issues are decided. In the next chapter, we turn to the federal laws that most directly impact the work of the collections person.

Chapter 2
Collection Laws

Introduction

Several laws have been passed that apply, either directly or indirectly, to the collection function, mostly in regard to the protection of individuals. In this chapter, we provide an overview of the laws and their essential provisions. A collections person needs to be aware of these laws when conducting the collection activities described in the following chapters.

Consumer Credit Protection Act

Title III of the CCPA limits the amount of earnings that can be garnished from a person's paycheck to settle a past-due debt. The restriction is 25% of disposable weekly income after mandatory deductions for taxes or the amount by which disposable earnings are greater than 30 times the minimum wage. In effect, the Act keeps creditors from garnishing an unacceptably large amount of a person's wages, though it does allow a higher garnishment percentage for past-due taxes and child support payments.

Some states have enacted more restrictions on garnishments, such as exempting the wages of a head of household from any type of garnishment.

Fair Debt Collection Practices Act

The FDCPA is the law with the most immediate impact on the collections function. Its provisions are intended to protect individuals, not businesses. Also, the Act is intended to apply to third party collection agencies and attorneys, but has been applied at the state level to the activities of original creditors. It applies only to the collection of debt incurred by a consumer primarily for personal, family, or household purposes. It does not apply to the collection of corporate debt or debt owed for business or agricultural purposes. Key provisions of the Act are as follows:

- *Additional charges*. The collector is not allowed to collect bad check charges or service charges unless these amounts were expressly authorized in the underlying debt agreement, and are allowed by the applicable state law.
- *Attorney contacts*. If a collector knows that a consumer has retained an attorney to handle a debt and can easily ascertain the attorney's contact information, then all contacts must be with the attorney, unless the attorney is unresponsive or allows direct communication with the consumer.
- *Caller identification*. A collector must disclose himself or herself to the contacted consumer at the beginning of a call. It is possible to use an alias, as long as the alias used can be traced to a real person.
- *Calling behavior*. A collector is not allowed to call repeatedly with the intent of annoying an individual, or to contact them at their place of employment (if

prohibited by the employer), or to contact them when an attorney is representing them. Threats or abusive language are also not allowed. There is no legal clarification at the federal level of how many calls per day or month are considered acceptable.

- *Calling hours.* A collector is limited to calling within the hours of 8 a.m. to 9 p.m. local time.
- *Credit report.* The filing of false information with a credit agency about an individual is not allowed.
- *Deception.* Misrepresenting oneself in order to collect a debt (such as claiming to be a police officer, attorney, or government official) is not allowed. It is also considered deceptive to state that nonpayment will result in a consumer's arrest or imprisonment. Further, it is illegal to send simulated legal documents to a consumer, implying that a legal complaint has been filed when this is not really the case.
- *Disclosure statement.* The collector must state "This is an attempt to collect the debt and any information will be used for that purpose" in all communications with a consumer. This statement should be made in both written and oral communications. Any communication must also state that it is from a debt collector.
- *False representations.* A collector cannot falsely represent that nonpayment will result in the arrest of anyone, or that assets will be seized or wages garnished, unless such action is lawful and intended by the collector.[1] It is also not acceptable to falsely state why the caller is trying to locate a consumer, such as by stating that the consumer has just received an inheritance and an address is needed to send the person the money.
- *Governmental communication format.* It is illegal to falsely use a return address or the form or shape of envelopes that appear to indicate that a communication originates from a governmental office.
- *Halt communications.* A collector is required to cease communications with an individual if the person requests it in writing. At this point, the collector can notify the consumer of subsequent steps to be taken, such as the repossession of a vehicle.
- *Justification.* A collector is not allowed to demand amounts that have not been justified.
- *Location of contacts.* If calling a consumer at the person's place of work, ask if this is an acceptable time to talk, and verify that coworkers cannot overhear the call. If the employer prohibits personal calls, then terminate the call at once. It is generally inadvisable to call a consumer at his or her place of work.
- *Property repossession.* A collector cannot threaten to repossess or disable property when the creditor has no right to the property.

---

[1] It is generally not possible for a collector to seize a debtor's household furniture and personal effects, nor the income from pension and retirement funds. The details vary by state. Exemptions are especially broad when a debtor resides in Florida, where there is an exemption of up to 160 acres and no minimum dollar amount on a primary residence.

- *Publication of debt information.* A collector cannot publish a list of consumers who do not pay their debts, nor can the collector advertise these debts for sale.
- *Third party contacts.* A collector is not allowed to discuss the nature of a debt with other parties (other than to obtain contact information), or to publish a person's name and location, or to use any form of communication that would make the debt information available to the public (such as sending an overdue notice on a post card or stating that the firm is a debt collector on its return address on an envelope). Prohibited communications include discussions of the debt owed with friends and relatives of the consumer, as well as neighbors, roommates, and housekeepers.

Tip: Contacting a consumer via email is generally not recommended, since a third party (such as a family member) could access the consumer's computer and open the message. This constitutes a third-party disclosure, which is prohibited by the Act.

- *Use of another name.* A collector must use the true name of the debt collector's organization. The use of any other name is prohibited.
- *Validation of debts.* A collector must provide the consumer with certain basic information, including the amount of the debt, the name of the creditor, and notice that the consumer has 30 days to dispute the debt before it is assumed to be valid.

Note: The FDCPA *does* apply to a creditor that controls the collection agency or law firm that is contacting debtors on its behalf.

When a debt collector does not comply with the provisions of this Act, the collector is liable for any actual damages sustained as a result of that failure, as well as punitive damages of up to $1,000 in an individual action. In a class action, punitive damages are up to $1,000 for each plaintiff and an award to be divided among all members of the class of an amount up to $500,000 or one percent of the debt collector's net worth, whichever is less. A collector can avoid liability by proving that any violation of the Act was unintentional, resulting from a bona fide error. This defense can be supported by the ongoing use of a procedures manual, on-the-job training, and telephonic monitoring, showing that the collector has a robust system in place for complying with the Act.

Though the Act is intended to only limit the actions of collection agencies, the collections manager could incorporate its provisions into the in-house collection procedure, on the grounds that the provisions of the Act are fair and reasonable.

Note: A collection agency will not be considered subject to this Act when it is not meaningfully involved in the collection of debts. This situation arises when it is only acting as a mailing service for a creditor, or where it is only being paid for sending letters, rather than as a percentage of the debts collected, or when the collection agency is not allowed to initiate any phone calls to the debtor, or when the collection agency has no authority to negotiate the amount of debt collected.

Service Members Civil Relief Act (SMCRA)

The SMCRA applies to all members of the military services, and affords the following protections to them:

- *Capped interest rate.* If a service member has a credit obligation, the interest rate on it is limited to six percent while the person is on active duty. If the debt is a mortgage, the reduced rate extends for one year after active-duty service. This reduced rate applies to credit card debts, car loans, business obligations, some student loans and other debts, as well as fees, service charges and renewal fees.
- *Deferred income taxes.* All taxing authorities must defer income taxes due before or during a person's military service, if the person's ability to pay the income tax is materially affected by military service. No interest or penalty can be added because of this deferral.
- *Eviction prevention.* A person cannot be evicted for nonpayment of rent without a court order; this protection applies to residences where the monthly rent is below a certain threshold level.
- *Postponement of foreclosures.* No sale, foreclosure, or seizure of property for nonpayment of a mortgage is valid if made during or within nine months after a person's service on active duty, unless carrying out a valid court order.
- *Prevention of property repossession.* Property cannot be repossessed for nonpayment or a contract terminated for any payment gaps prior to or during military service without a court order.
- *Protection against default judgments.* If a civil action is filed against a person on active duty, the judge must appoint a lawyer to represent the person. In addition, the court must grant a stay of at least 90 days if it determines that there may be a defense to the action, and the defense cannot be presented without the person's attendance.
- *Protection for small business owners.* The nonbusiness assets and military pay of a small business owner are protected from creditors while a person is on active duty. This applies to business debts and other obligations.
- *Termination of automobile lease.* A person can terminate an automobile lease when the lease was signed prior to being called to active duty, or when the lease was signed prior to receiving permanent change-of-station orders outside the continental United States, or signed a lease and then received orders to deploy.

- *Termination of residential lease*. A person can terminate his or her residential lease, as well as other types of leases, including agricultural, professional and business, by delivering a written notice of termination. This applies when the person entered into a lease and then started military service, or entered into a lease during service and then received permanent change of station orders.

If a creditor intends to litigate against a former service member, the creditor bears the burden of proving that the individual is no longer on active service.

The net effect of the SMCRA is that collection activities against members of the military are more difficult to pursue than is the case for other individuals.

Telephone Consumer Protection Act (TCPA)

The following actions are expressly prohibited under the TCPA unless the targeted individual has already given consent:

- *Automated calls*. Solicitors cannot send messages to residences that employ a recorded message[2]. These calls also cannot be sent to cell phones, 911 emergency numbers, hospital emergency numbers, a physician's office, or similar recipients.
- *Call times*. A solicitor is not allowed to call a private residence prior to 8 a.m. or after 9 p.m., local time.
- *Do-not-call list*. A solicitor must maintain an in-house list of consumers that have requested that they not be called, and have a policy for properly maintaining it. In addition, solicitors must observe the list of consumers noted on the national do-not-call registry.
- *Faxes*. Advertising faxes cannot be sent unless the recipient has expressly allowed them.
- *Identification*. The solicitor must identify himself, the name of the entity on whose behalf the call is being made, and provide contact information.

> **Tip:** The use of a policies and procedures manual, as well as ongoing in-house training, is recommended to ensure that the soliciting entity complies with all aspects of the Act.

A solicitor can avoid the TCPA by manually dialing calls, since the Act is directed at auto-dialing systems. In short, the Act is restricting auto-dialing technology, rather than the form of communication.

Note that a "solicitor" as stated in the preceding list also means a collector. Someone receiving a telephone call in violation of this act can sue for up to $1,500 per violation, and can seek an injunction to prevent further calls.

---

[2] A solicitor can leave a pre-recorded message, but must first obtain the express consent of the party to be called. Proof of such consent includes a written agreement, a telephone recording, a text message, fax, or letter. This consent can be revoked by any reasonable means.

Summary

Because of the various laws noted in this chapter, a collections person should be vigilant in the following areas:

- *Behavior boundaries*. Establish clear boundaries of acceptable behavior for the collection staff that keep the organization from being liable under any laws, and monitor the collectors to ensure that they comply with these restrictions. Since the actions of collection agencies could be construed as the actions of the creditor, enforce these same boundaries with any agencies that work for the company.
- *Monitoring*. There are ongoing updates to several of the laws, so have someone with legal experience monitor the updates and determine how they may impact the company's collection operations. Also monitor any variations on these laws at the state level.
- *Procedures*. Periodically review and adjust the firm's procedures that are impacted by these laws, and train the staff regarding the updates. Also, have an attorney review the procedures to ensure that they comply with the law.

Chapter 3
Credit Transactions

Introduction

A business may engage in a number of credit transactions. From a collection perspective, one must have a clear understanding of the mechanics of real property financing and personal property financing, including such matters as guaranty and surety arrangements, security interests, and claim priorities – all of which are covered in this chapter.

Credit Concepts

When someone wants to make a large purchase, it may be necessary to do so on credit, where the lending party is known as a lender or creditor. The party taking on the debt is called the borrower or debtor.

EXAMPLE

Rapunzel Hair Products borrows $25,000 from Currency Bank. In this relationship, Rapunzel is the borrower and Currency Bank is the lender.

A lender can elect to extend unsecured credit to a borrower. When this is the case, the lender is not requiring the borrower to provide any collateral. *Collateral* is an asset or group of assets that a borrower has pledged as security for a loan. The lender has the legal right to seize and sell the asset(s) if the borrower is unable to pay back the loan by the agreed date. An example of collateral is a house bought with a mortgage. If the amount realized from the lender's sale of collateral still does not pay off the remaining balance on a loan, then the lender can sue the borrower for the remaining amount.

In an unsecured loan, the lender is taking a chance that the borrower will make good on its promise to pay back the loan principal and any associated interest. This is more common when a lender is dealing with a large, established customer that has a proven record of reliably paying back its loans. In many cases, it is not possible for a borrower to obtain a loan without collateral.

Note: There is no collateral associated with credit card debt, which (in part) explains the high interest rates charged by credit card providers.

EXAMPLE

Jim borrows $7,000 from Terrence. Terrence extends the loan without demanding any collateral for the loan, relying instead on Jim's positive cash flow when he makes the loan. If Jim defaults on the arrangement, Terrence will have no collateral to fall back on, and will instead have to sue for recovery of the unpaid loan balance.

To avoid the scenario described in the preceding example, most lenders require a security interest in a borrower's property. When this happens, the lender is known as a *secured creditor*.

Real Property Financing

Real property is land and everything permanently attached to it. When an owner of real property borrows money, the lender may demand that the property be designated as collateral on the loan, which is called a *mortgage*.

EXAMPLE

Epic Rest Hotels wants to acquire land and build a hotel on it. To do so, it borrows $12 million from General Bank. In this arrangement, General Bank is the lender and Epic Risk is the borrower. To secure the loan, General demands a mortgage on the land and hotel. This constitutes a secured loan, with the property being used as collateral. If Epic Rest defaults on its loan payments, the bank can take possession of the property.

Under the laws of most states, a mortgage must be recorded at the county recorder's office in the county where the property is located. This results in a public record that a mortgage has been recorded against the specified property. This recordation is useful for lenders in general, who search county recorder records to determine whether there are any existing liens on a property.

If a lender neglects to record a mortgage at the county recorder's office, the mortgage is still valid, but it will not be legally effective against any subsequent purchasers of the property, or against other lien holders.

EXAMPLE

Zachary buys a home for $800,000. To finance it, he borrows $600,000 from Currency Bank. Through a clerical error, Currency Bank does not record the mortgage with the applicable county recorder's office. Zachary then applies to Hamilton Bank for a $200,000 loan. Hamilton finds no mortgage recorded against the property, and so loans the $200,000 to Zachary and properly records its mortgage with the county recorder's office. A few months later, Zachary defaults on both loans. Hamilton Bank can seize the house, since it recorded the mortgage and Currency Bank did not. Currency Bank can still sue Zachary for recovery of the unpaid portion of the loan.

Once a mortgage has been fully repaid, the lender files a satisfaction of mortgage document with the county recorder's office, stating that the mortgage has been paid.

A borrower is considered to be in default when scheduled payments are not made. When this involves a mortgage, the lender can trigger a foreclosure action to seize the property. If a court agrees, then it will issue a judgment, mandating that the property be sold. If the proceeds of this sale exceed the residual balance of the underlying loan, then the excess amount must be forwarded to the borrower.

In some states, the foreclosure and property sale procedure can be built into a mortgage agreement, with no need to bring the matter to a court for resolution. When this approach is used, state governments mandate that the property must be sold at auction, in order to obtain the highest possible price.

EXAMPLE

Doug borrows $675,000 from Hamilton Bank to acquire a property, with the property serving as collateral. A few years later, Doug defaults on the loan when $600,000 of the loan principal has not yet been paid. Hamilton Bank forecloses on the property and sells it for $630,000. The bank can retain $600,000 and must forward the remaining $30,000 to Doug.

Depending on the applicable state law, it may be possible for a lender to obtain a deficiency judgment from a court when the amount it collects from a foreclosure sale does not equal the remaining balance on a loan. This means that the lender can recover the remaining amount from the borrower's other property.

Some states permit a borrower to redeem real property after a loan default has occurred, but before it has been foreclosed. Under these right of redemption rules, the borrower must pay back all the remaining principal, as well as any interest due and other costs incurred by the lender because of the default event.

Mechanic's Liens

Many contractors may be called upon to work on a property, including bricklayers, carpenters, electricians, and roofers. These contractors put both their own labor and significant amounts of materials into improving a property. The amounts these contractors have invested can be protected by mechanic's liens under state law. These liens are filed against the property on which a contractor worked by filing them at the applicable county recorder's office. By doing so, the property becomes security for payments due to a contractor. This is a contractor's equivalent to having a mortgage on a property. Consequently, if a property owner defaults on payments due to a contractor, the contractor can foreclose on the lien and sell the property in order to obtain restitution for the amounts owed.

A property owner can request that contractors sign a lien release document, which releases any lien that they might file against the owner's property. In this case, the only recourse of a contractor is to sue the property owner for recovery of the amount due.

> **Tip:** A mechanic's lien may expire after a fixed period of time, so keep track of the expiration date and renew it at regular intervals.

Guaranty Arrangements

When a borrower has poor credit fundamentals, a lender may refuse to lend any money unless an outside party with better credit agrees to become liable for repayment of the loan. In essence, the better credit of this outside party becomes the security that the lender needs in order to issue a loan. There are two variations on the concept, which are addressed in the following bullet points:

- *Guarantee arrangement.* In this arrangement, a third party agrees to pay a loan if the borrower defaults. This person is secondarily liable for the loan, after the borrower. This means that the lender must first attempt to collect the debt from the borrower, and only then can pursue the guarantor for payment.
- *Surety arrangement.* In this arrangement, a third party agrees to be liable for repayment of a borrower's loan. This person is effectively a co-signer on the loan, since the lender can seek repayment from the surety even when the primary borrower is not in default on the loan.

EXAMPLE

Orlando has just graduated from college and obtained a job, so he needs a car to commute to work. A lender will not extend him the credit to buy the car, since he has no credit history. In order to issue a loan, the lender requires Orlando's parents to co-sign the loan, making them a surety. After a few months, Orlando loses his job and defaults on the loan, so the lender brings a legal action against Orlando's parents to pay for the loan.

Collection Options

There are several possible collection options available to a lender when a borrower defaults on its payments. Consider the following alternatives:

- *Writ of attachment.* A pre-judgment writ of attachment can be ordered in a legal action in which a plaintiff has demonstrated that fraud exists, or that the defendant may attempt to dispose of or hide assets from the court. In this situation, a prejudgment writ of attachment functions as a temporary restraining order, which preserves assets held by the defendant pending a final resolution of the dispute, so that the plaintiff can recover its losses from sale of the assets. While it is in effect, the defendant cannot use or dispose of the assets. The downside of using this approach is that a plaintiff must post a surety bond of up to two times the fair value of the property seized. The defendant can file a counter bond to release the attachment, giving it use of the underlying asset(s). This option is not available in many states.

> **Tip:** A plaintiff should not use a writ of attachment unless there is a high degree of certainty regarding the success of the associated lawsuit. Otherwise, the defendant can sue for damages.

- *Writ of execution.* This option allows a lender to seize a borrower's property. If approved by a court, the local sheriff is directed to seize the debtor's property, after which a sale of the property is conducted. The proceeds from this sale are then used to pay back the lender. Any overage from the sale is returned to the borrower. A writ of execution is needed when a lender wins a court judgment against a borrower, and the borrower refuses to pay the amount of the judgment.
- *Writ of garnishment.* This option allows a lender to seize property of a borrower that is held by a third party, via a garnishment. A garnishment frequently involves court orders to employers to retain the wages of their employees to pay for child support, unpaid taxes, and unpaid debts. Employers are then required to remit these wages to the applicable court or creditor. There are limitations on the proportion of a person's wages that can be garnished.

Personal Property Financing

Personal property refers to any assets other than land or buildings. Personal property is movable, and so can include such assets as computers, equipment, furniture, home appliances, and vehicles. These are all examples of tangible personal property. There is also *in*tangible personal property, which includes copyrights, patents, trademarks, and securities.

The more expensive personal property items are routinely sold on credit. This may be in the form of unsecured credit, in which case the personal property being acquired is not used as collateral to secure the underlying loan. Instead, the lender bases its lending decision on the credit rating of the borrower. In cases where there is no collateral, a lender will need to sue the borrower to recover the unpaid amount of a loan.

For more expensive personal property, a lender will require that an asset be pledged as collateral on a loan. In this case, the lender can seek to seize the asset being used as collateral if a borrower defaults on loan payments.

A personal property financing situation can involve either two or three parties. When just two are involved, the seller is selling goods on credit directly to a customer, while retaining a security (collateral) interest in the goods. When three parties are involved, the seller is selling goods to a customer who is financing the purchase with funds obtained from a lender; in this case, the lender takes a security interest in the goods.

EXAMPLE

A furniture hobbyist buys a lathe from a machine tool manufacturer, which also finances the purchases. The manufacturer retains a security interest in the lathe, which is the collateral on the loan extended to the hobbyist.

Alternatively, the hobbyist could have obtained the necessary financing from a bank, and then used the funds to buy the lathe. In this case, it is the bank that obtains a security interest in the lathe.

Security Interests in Personal Property

In this section, we cover the key elements of a security interest, including its initial creation, then perfecting the interest, and then using it to obtain remedies for borrower nonpayment.

Creating a Security Interest

When a lender wants to create a security interest in the personal property of a borrower, the first step in doing so is to obtain a signed security agreement from the borrower. This agreement must contain the following information:

- *Description*. It must describe the personal property in sufficient detail to identify it.
- *Lender's rights*. It must state the rights of the lender in the event of a default by the borrower.
- *Promise to repay*. It must contain the details of the borrower's promise to repay, including the amount, timing of payments, and interest rate.
- *Signature*. It must contain the borrower's signature.

Tip: Itemize every personal property item in the security agreement. Otherwise, a more general description such as "All debtor equipment located at 123 Main Street" will be rendered useless if the debtor moves to a new location or shifts some of the property to a different location.

Once this agreement has been signed, the lender has an enforceable security interest against the borrower, and has a legal right to pay off the outstanding debt from the identified collateral. Further, if the borrower sells the collateral identified in this agreement, then the lender can legally obtain the sale proceeds. Similarly, if the borrower exchanges the collateral for different assets, then the lender has the right to seize the replacement assets.

A variation on this basic agreement is to state that the lender's security interest will attach to additional property that was not initially owned by the borrower when the agreement was signed. This is called a *floating lien*.

EXAMPLE

Laid Back Corporation borrows $180,000 from Third Central Bank and provides it with a security interest in both its current inventory of business chairs and what it will acquire during the term of the loan. If Laid Back defaults on its payments, then Third Central can satisfy its security claim by taking not only any remaining original inventory, but also inventory that was acquired later.

A variation on the security interest concept is applied to a line of credit. In a line of credit arrangement, a borrower can repeatedly draw down and pay back a fixed amount of credit over a designated lending period. As part of this arrangement, the borrower designates certain items of personal property to be collateral against the loan for its duration. This approach keeps the lender from having to execute a new security agreement every time the borrower draws down the line of credit.

EXAMPLE

Monique Ponto, maker of fine women's watches, enters into a $5 million line of credit arrangement with Currency Bank, and pledges its watch inventory as security for all drawdowns of the line of credit. Monique then draws down $1.3 million, which is secured by the inventory. The company pays it back a few months later, and then draws down another $700,000. This second borrowing is also secured by the inventory.

A secured party can release a portion of the collateral identified on a security agreement by modifying the agreement. This change can be useful when negotiating with a debtor for the partial payment of an amount due.

Perfecting a Security Interest

A secured lender will need to establish its rights over any other secured creditors that might claim an interest in a borrower's collateral. There are three ways to do so. The first option is to file a *financing statement* with the applicable government office, which is also the most common approach. This is usually done on the UCC Filing Statement (Form UCC-1). It may be possible to electronically file this form, depending on the systems used by the local government. The form is usually filed with the county recorder's office. A financing statement will only be enforceable when it contains the name of the borrower, the name and address of the lender, and the collateral being covered by it. The statement will then be enforceable for a period of five years from the filing date, after which the lender can file a continuation statement to extend the term of the financing statement for an additional five years. Once a secured debt has been paid, the lender must file a termination statement with the government office where the financing statement was originally filed. This must be done within one month of when the debt was paid.

The second option for establishing a lender's rights is to take possession of the collateral. When this is done, there is no need to also file a financing statement. When a lender takes possession, it is required to be reasonably careful in preserving the collateral.

EXAMPLE

Linda borrows $6,000 from Michael and hands over her camper van as collateral. Michael does not file a financing statement. A local bank obtains a judgment against Linda for nonpayment of another loan. The bank cannot recover the camper van from Michael, despite his lack of a financing statement. Michael's possession of the camper van perfects his security interest in it.

The third option for establishing a lender's rights is via a purchase money security interest. This approach is used by a seller that is extending credit to a customer that is buying consumer goods, such as furniture or home appliances. The customer signs the agreement at the point of sale, which immediately perfects the seller's interest in the associated goods. There is no need for the seller to take possession of the goods or file a financing statement.

EXAMPLE

Grunge Motor Sports sells one of its Caveman XT dirt bikes to Fred for $5,000, on credit. Grunge requires Fred to sign a security agreement, which means that Grunge now has a purchase money security interest in the dirt bike that is perfected as soon as Fred signs the agreement.

When a buyer in the ordinary course of business acquires goods from a merchant, the buyer is acquiring them free of any security interest. A buyer in the ordinary course of business is someone who purchases goods in good faith from a seller who is in the business of selling these types of goods.

EXAMPLE

Amalgamated Farm Products, which sells tractors, finances its tractor inventory through a loan from AgriBank. The bank takes a security interest in Amalgamated's tractor inventory and perfects its security interest. Farmer John, a buyer in the ordinary course of business, buys a tractor from Amalgamated for cash. In the event of a default by Amalgamated, the bank cannot recover the tractor from Farmer John.

Tip: When a patent is being used as collateral, hire a patent attorney to file the security interest with the United States Patent and Trademark Office, in addition to the normal UCC filing.

Garage Keeper Liens

Depending on the state, the owner of a vehicle repair facility can assert a lien on any vehicle on which the garage completed repairs. The owner can sell the vehicle in order to obtain payment for the unpaid repair bill; however, the vehicle owner must first be warned of the upcoming sale. Various state laws allow the vehicle owner to then contest the lien before a vehicle is sold.

If a vehicle being sold under a garage keeper's lien is leased, the lessor must provide its consent before the vehicle can be sold.

Claim Priority

It is possible that several lenders will claim an interest in the same collateral. Two factors determine which lender will prevail. The first factor is whether a claim is secured; the claim that is secured will prevail. If there are several secured claims, then the claim that was filed first will prevail. However, these general rules do not address all possible scenarios. The following listing presents a variety of claim priority situations:

1. A security interest prevails over any unsecured interest.
2. When there are several security interests, the one with a perfected claim will prevail.
3. When there are several perfected security interests, the first to perfect will prevail.
4. When there is a perfected security interest, but the identified goods are later mixed in with other goods for which there are also perfected security interests, all of these interests are assumed to be equal.

Remedies

When a borrower has not made scheduled payments when due or has declared bankruptcy, a lending arrangement is usually considered to be in default (the exact circumstances will depend on the terms included in a lending arrangement). When this happens, the lender can select from the following options for remedies:

*   *Retain the collateral*. The lender may repossess and retain the goods being used as collateral, in complete satisfaction of the debt. The lender must notify the borrower of its intention to retain the collateral.
*   *Sell the collateral*. The lender may repossess and sell the goods being used as collateral, and settle the debt from the proceeds of that sale. The lender must notify the borrower in writing of the time and place of the sale. Any surplus garnered from the sale is paid to the borrower.
*   *Deficiency judgment*. If the lender does not obtain enough cash from the sale of collateral to satisfy the debt, and if the borrower is personally liable for the debt, then the lender can sue to recover a deficiency judgment against the borrower.

- *Relinquish security interest*. If the value of the collateral has declined precipitously, the lender may elect to relinquish its security interest and instead proceed directly to a judgment against the borrower to recover the remaining amount due. This approach is only used when the borrower is known to have sufficient assets to pay off the debt balance.

> **Tip:** A creditor frequently has a repossession agent repossess goods on its behalf. Be aware that the creditor can be held responsible for any breach of the peace caused by this party. It can be useful to include in the agreement with the repossession agent a clause requiring the agent to reimburse the creditor for any fines associated with a breach of the peace.

EXAMPLE

Trevor borrows $72,000 from Motor Bank to buy an antique car. He signs a security agreement, giving the bank a purchase money security interest in the vehicle. Trevor makes a number of payments to reduce the loan balance to $54,000, and then defaults. Motor Bank repossesses the car and sells it at an antique car auction for $50,000. The selling expenses of $4,000 are deducted from the proceeds of the auction, leaving $46,000 that is applied to the remaining loan balance. The residual $8,000 on the loan is a personal liability that Motor Bank can pursue against Trevor.

A borrower has the right to redeem collateral before the lender has sold it or exercised a right to retain it. This right can only be exercised by paying all obligations due, including any related legal and collection costs of the lender.

> **Tip:** A creditor that has repossessed assets and which plans to sell them has an obligation to do so relatively quickly. Otherwise, it will run up storage fees, and the assets may decline in value. In this situation, a court may not allow the creditor to collect any deficiencies still remaining once the assets have been sold.

> **Tip:** When selling repossessed assets, always obtain the name and address of everyone attending the public auction, in order to prove that a reasonable price was obtained in a competitive bidding situation.

Summary

There are very specific recovery rights available to a lender. They vary based on the types of assets associated with a loan, as well as whether the lender has taken a security interest in collateral, whether that interest has been perfected, and the timing of the filing. These issues are most important to a business that routinely engages in lending; in these situations, a firm should have rock-solid procedures in place for processing debt-related paperwork, so that it does not lose its rights in relation to collateral, and understands its options for obtaining repayment from borrowers.

Chapter 4
Legal Issues Associated
with Collection Activities

Introduction

In this chapter, we address the legal issues associated with various collection activities. The discussion is wide-ranging, including specific changes to the credit application form to enhance a creditor's ability to collect overdue funds, how to deal with bounced checks, a bank's right of setoff, piercing the corporate veil, and much more.

Credit Application Upgrades

There are several ways to upgrade a credit application in order to improve the chances of collecting from a customer. The following bullet points are intended to improve the legal position of the creditor:

- *Identify the applicant's form of business.* How to collect a debt depends on the form of business being used by a credit applicant. For example, it is permissible to pursue the personal assets of the owner of a sole proprietor, whereas this is not the case when the applicant is a corporation. Therefore, the application should mandate that the applicant state whether it is a sole proprietorship, partnership, or some form of corporation.
- *Identify owners.* In the case of a general partnership, include on the credit application a requirement for all partners to include their contact information. This information can be used to pursue the partners individually for repayment, since the partners are liable for the obligations of the partnership. Or, if the applicant is a sole proprietorship, require that the owner enter his or her name, address, and phone number.
- *Identify the corporate parent.* If the applicant is a subsidiary, ask for the name and address of the parent company. This information is useful when an attempt is made to hold affiliated corporations jointly liable for a debt.

> **Tip:** Do not allow the entry of a post office box in a credit application, since a summons cannot be served upon such an address.

- *Specify the business name.* In order to pursue a debt in court, the creditor must use the correct name. Therefore, clearly state on the application that the applicant must provide its business name, as opposed to its trade name.
- *Identify the bank account.* Be sure to ask for the name of the bank where the applicant maintains an account. This information may be needed later, if the creditor obtains a judgment and wants to attach the bank account.

- *Venue.* The credit application should list the state within which any litigation is to be conducted. The state should be the location most convenient for the creditor, not the customer. The customer must sign the credit application, thereby agreeing to the designated venue.
- *Interest and penalty policy.* State on all credit applications, invoices, dunning letters, and other communications with customers that the creditor charges interest on overdue account balances. The attorney can use these documents as evidence that an interest charge is an integral part of the arrangement between the creditor and the customer, which makes it more likely that an interest charge can be added to the creditor's claim.

Legal Solutions for Bounced Checks

When a customer's check payment to a seller bounces, the solutions available to the seller will depend on the applicable state law. The typical state will allow the holder of a bounced check to recover from the debtor the costs associated with the transaction, including attorney's fees. Also, depending on the state, it may be possible to collect double or even triple damages if the situation meets the requirements set forth in the applicable state law.

The Fair Debt Collection Practices Act allows a creditor to charge the debtor a bounced check fee, as long as the creditor includes this right in its agreement with the debtor. Some state laws allow the creditor to charge the debtor the actual bounced check fee incurred by the creditor, while others allow for the billing of a specific amount, perhaps with an upper cap, such as $100. In order to charge customers across state lines the correct fee, a seller would need to know the applicable state laws pertaining to the allowable fees for bounced checks.

> **Tip:** It may not be cost-effective to charge bounced check fees to debtors, if doing so requires an inordinate amount of administrative time to keep track of state-level rules regarding these fees.

Acceptance of a Lesser Check Amount

A debtor may dispute the amount billed to it and offers to settle for a lesser amount, sending the creditor a check payment that contains a value less than the billed amount. If the creditor elects to deposit this check, then it has accepted the offered settlement amount, and no longer has a claim on the debtor. Alternatively, it can elect to return the check and pursue full payment.

> **Tip:** Make the cash receipts clerk aware of the consequences of cashing any received checks that state "payment in full," "in full settlement," or similar text. These checks should always be referred to a supervisor before being deposited.

The situation is more complex when a debtor is disputing a billing issued to it by a larger business, where the seller has multiple departments. In this case, someone in the collections department of the creditor might be aware of the dispute, but not the cash receipts department. In this case, the rule is that the debtor cannot send a "payment in full" check to the creditor and have its debt discharged if the following conditions are present:

- The payee is an organization;
- The organization has communicated to the debtor that a "payment in full" offer be sent to a particular location or person; and
- The check was not received by the designated location or person.

In this situation, the check is considered a partial payment, rather than a payment in full.

A Bank's Right of Setoff

Once a judgment has been obtained against a creditor, a common collection tactic is to attach the creditor's bank account, thereby gaining immediate access to what may be sufficient funds to settle the debt in question. However, the bank at which the account is held may have issued a loan to the debtor, in which case the bank may have a right of setoff against the account. This means that the bank can extract funds from the account in order to settle the outstanding amount of the debt. A right of setoff is superior to any judgment obtained by a creditor, so it is quite possible that attaching a debtor's bank account will not have a happy result for the creditor.

Collecting on Guarantees

When one party guarantees the debt of another, it must be in writing. This arrangement is between the guarantor and the party that is extending credit to a third party. The guarantor will only be required to pay the creditor if the original borrower fails to pay the debt. This situation commonly arises when the parents of a young adult assist that person in his or her purchase of a vehicle. The creditor will not extend credit, since the borrower does not yet have a credit history. As long as the parents agree in writing to pay if the son or daughter does not pay, the creditor will agree to grant credit.

> **Note:** When the main point of a guarantee arrangement is to provide a benefit to the guarantor, then the agreement does not have to be in writing.

EXAMPLE

George is the sole owner of Smithy Ironworks. Smithy borrows $50,000 from the Midas Industrial Bank, and George orally guarantees that he will personally repay the debt if Smithy cannot. Midas can enforce this promise, since the loan will benefit George, as the sole shareholder.

When a contract that is required to be in writing is not, it is generally unenforceable. In cases where an oral contract that should have been in writing has already been completed, then neither party to it can rescind the contract.

Piercing the Corporate Veil

When a debtor is a corporation, its shareholders are shielded from liability. However, this may not be the case in certain circumstances, allowing creditors to access the assets of shareholders. This is known as piercing the corporate veil. Piercing the veil can be accomplished in the following three situations:

- *No separation between the corporation and its owners.* If the owners have failed to maintain a formal legal separation between a business and their personal financial affairs, a court may find that the firm is just a sham, and that the owners are personally operating it as though the corporation did not exist. This situation can arise when the owner of a company pays his personal bills from the entity's checking account.
- *Corporate actions are fraudulent or wrongful.* If the owners of a company have recklessly borrowed and lost money, made business deals knowing that the firm could not pay the bills, or otherwise acted recklessly or dishonestly, a court could conclude that fraud was perpetrated.
- *Creditors suffered an unmerited cost.* If someone who transacted business with the company is stuck with unpaid invoices or an unpaid court judgment, and the preceding factors are present, a court may find this to be adequate grounds to pierce the corporate veil

A corporate parent may park assets in a subsidiary in an effort to hide the assets from creditors. Creditors will want to look for indicators that this is the case, so that they can attempt to pierce the corporate veil. Indicators are that the subsidiary is seriously under-capitalized, shares board members and employees with its parent, pays no rent, has no separate logo or stationery, and rarely sends funds to the parent.

Reverse piercing is also possible. This is when a corporation is held liable for the obligations of its owners.

Dealing with Agents

An *agent* is an individual or business that acts on behalf of another party. The agent's authority may be express (via an agreement) or implied. An agent can trigger a liability for the principal when acting within the scope of its responsibilities for the principal. Examples of agents are sales representatives and shipping agents, as are the officers of a corporation. When dealing with an agent, the relationship is essentially with the principal being represented. In order to ensure that the agent is truly representing the principal, it makes sense to obtain a written authorization from the principal. Alternatively, it is possible to rely on the apparent authority of the agent to act on behalf of the principal. Apparent authority is present when a principal expressly or implicitly authorizes the conduct of an agent.

This is a significant issue in collection law, since an agent could place an order with a seller, which the seller relies on to issue an invoice to the principal, which then refuses to pay.

EXAMPLE

An office manager orders raw materials for the production operations of her employer. The creditor ships the raw materials to the employer, which retains the raw materials but does not pay on the grounds that the office manager is not authorized to order raw materials. An argument can be made that the office manager at least has the apparent authority to order office supplies, though it is an arguable point that her apparent authority does not extend to the purchase of raw materials. At a minimum, the seller can pursue payment on the grounds of unjust enrichment[3], since the buying party cannot keep the raw materials and yet not pay for them.

Assignment of Debt Situations

A creditor may assign its debt to a third party. This happens when a business sells its accounts receivable to a finance company in exchange for an immediate discounted payment. In this situation, the creditor has an obligation to notify the debtor that payment should now be sent to the assignee. This notification should be in writing, to provide evidence that notice was made. At that point, if the debtor persists in paying the assignor, then the assignee can file a claim for wrongful payment against both the debtor and the assignor.

If the debtor does not believe that the assignment was proper, then it can legally continue making payments to the assignor, rather than the assignee.

Assignment for the Benefit of Creditors

To avoid bankruptcy, a debtor may elect to transfer its assets to a trustee, who then converts the assets into cash and distributes the proceeds to the debtor's creditors in settlement of all debts. For creditors to collect funds from the trustee, they must submit a proof of claim. If there is a surplus remaining after this distribution, it is returned to the debtor. State law typically governs how the funds are to be distributed, with secured creditors taking precedence over general creditors.

In this situation, the debtor must send notice of the event to all creditors, though the creditors do not need to approve it. Creditors can also continue to take other collection steps to obtain payment, or to keep other creditors from being paid.

While this approach bears some similarities to bankruptcy, it is quicker and less expensive. On the downside, courts do not oversee any aspect of this assignment, so it can be abused by a debtor.

---

[3] Unjust enrichment arises when one party is enriched at the expense of another under circumstances that the law sees as unjust. When a party is deemed to be unjustly enriched, the law imposes an obligation upon the recipient to make restitution.

Note: An assignment for the benefit of creditors is not available in all states.

Vehicle Repossessions

The repossession of a vehicle by a creditor is permitted throughout the United States, but there are state-level restrictions that may apply to each individual situation. For example, some states require that a repossession notice be sent before the actual repossession can take place, while other states mandate that vehicle repossession cannot take place after a certain percentage of the payments have been made on a vehicle.

Tip: Be sure to maintain documentation of any repossession notices sent, in case the debtor objects to the subsequent vehicle repossession.

In most states, the creditor is held responsible for the actions of the party conducting vehicle repossessions on its behalf. Given the size of this potential liability, a creditor should conduct background checks on all repossession firms used, and obtain a copy of its insurance policies as they pertain to its repossession activities. The creditor should also have every repossession firm sign an agreement in which it indemnifies the creditor for any suits for damages related to the activities of the repossession firm.

Many states require that repossessions be peaceful. If the debtor is present, this means that the person peacefully surrenders the property. An ideal way to conduct a peaceful repossession is when a vehicle is parked on a street or in a public parking spot, where neither the debtor nor any of the person's friends or relatives are present. The worst-case scenario is to repossess a vehicle using threats or intimidation, since this is construed as a breach of the peace[4]. When it appears that a breach of the peace is possible, the persons conducting the repossession would be well advised to try again another time, when no one is present.

Note: The consent of the debtor is not required for repossession to occur, though the creditor should not enter a facility to repossess property without the consent of the person in charge.

In addition, some states require that the local firms physically engaged in repossession activities maintain a current collection agency license. The penalties for violating state law can be substantial, so be aware of local laws before engaging in vehicle repossession activities.

Tip: A threat to repossess a vehicle without actually intending to do so is a violation of the Fair Debt Collection Practices Act.

---

[4] A breach of the peace is a criminal offense that violates the public peace or order. Verbal or physical conduct indicating an objection to repossession can be considered a breach of the peace.

In cases where a repossession notice must be sent to a debtor prior to repossession, the triggering event is typically several missed payments – the exact number will vary by state.

Some creditors that have the right to repossess have elected not to in prior periods, allowing a debtor to be in arrears on one or more payments. In these situations, a court might construe the acceptance of late payments as a waiver of the repossession clause in a lending agreement. In these cases, the creditor should send a written notice by certified mail to the debtor, stating that strict compliance with the terms of the agreement will be required in the future if the debtor wants to avoid a vehicle repossession.

> **Tip:** Have an independent witness maintain a log of all personal possessions found in each repossessed vehicle, along with photographs of these items, to defend against any claims by debtors that personal property was stolen or damaged during the repossession.

When it becomes apparent that a debtor will not give up a vehicle peacefully, the creditor can instead obtain a court order to do so. If the debtor does not surrender the vehicle after being presented with the court order, the debtor can be held in contempt of court.

Receivership

A debtor may gradually drain the assets of a business, perhaps by selling them off at reduced prices or simply by not maintaining them in an adequate manner. For example, a landlord collects rent on a property, but does not use the proceeds to maintain the property. In this situation, a lender that obtains a judgment against the debtor can request that the court appoint a receiver of the assets. The receiver then takes possession of the assets, uses any cash inflows to maintain the property, and uses any surplus cash to pay off creditors.

Homestead Exemptions

The state governments have imposed a broad range of exemptions on the ability of a creditor to seize the household residence of a debtor. These homestead exemptions range from zero (Connecticut) to unlimited (Florida). In the case of large or unlimited exemptions, it can still make sense to examine the living arrangements of a debtor. Depending on the state, it may be possible to argue that a debtor should lose the household exemption because a business is being operated on the premises. The exemption may also be lost if the debtor is renting out the property, rather than living in it. Another possibility is that the homeowner conveyed the residence to a corporation; even if the homeowner owns 100% of the corporation, this action can void the homestead exemption.

Welfare and Social Security Income

A creditor cannot gain access to a debtor's welfare or social security income. This means that, if the income were to be deposited in a bank account, the creditor could not attach the account. This does not mean that a welfare or social security recipient is immune from the creditor – only that the creditor will need to pursue other income or assets, and not this income. Social security recipients in particular may earn income from other sources, which can be accessed by the creditor.

Summary

The intent of this chapter has been to focus on the legal aspects of certain collection techniques, rather than to provide a comprehensive set of collection tactics (for that information, see the author's *Effective Collections* manual). In all situations, be sure to explore the state-level laws that specifically apply to the case at hand before taking any action, since allowable collection activities can vary widely by state.

Chapter 5
The Collection Lawsuit

Introduction

A lawsuit will not be required to collect a debt in the vast majority of cases. When it *is* needed, the creditor should have a good knowledge of how the lawsuit process works and its role in achieving a successful conclusion – which we discuss in this chapter.

Litigation Advance Preparation

A creditor should prepare well in advance for the possibility that a claim over a receivable will end up in court. To do so, the business should consistently point out several legal issues to its customers, thereby establishing the ground rules for litigation. These and other issues are:

- *Notes and guarantees.* Whenever possible, obtain a signed note or personal guarantee to pay a debt. These documents establish the customer's commitment to pay the creditor. This is especially necessary when the customer's assets have already been mortgaged.
- *Acknowledgments.* Whenever possible, collectors should attempt to obtain written acknowledgments from customers that a debt exists. These documents can be admitted as evidence in court.
- *Proof of delivery.* Obtain from the freight carrier a proof of delivery, which can be used as evidence in court. Freight carriers may only issue such proof within a certain number of months of the delivery date, so be sure to obtain this evidence as soon as possible.
- *Security interest.* If the creditor has already filed a security interest in customer assets or goods shipped to a customer, it should periodically file continuation statements to ensure that the security interest is maintained.
- *Verify summons service address.* A service of summons can be made on a corporation by obtaining the address of the principal officer's residence, or by sending the summons to the relevant secretary of state (which forwards it to the corporation). When dealing with a partnership or sole proprietorship, the address of a partner or owner will be needed to serve the summons.

By consistently addressing these issues, a business provides its attorneys with a better set of tools for pursuing claims against customers.

Litigation Timing

Litigation has traditionally been considered the last possible option for collecting a debt, primarily because of its expense. However, being last on the list of collection activities does not mean that litigation should be excessively delayed. If a customer is in financial difficulties, its assets are dissipating by the day, so any delay reduces the chance of collection further. Consequently, as soon as all reasonable collection measures have been taken, turn an account over to an attorney.

One issue with litigation timing is the use of a collection agency. Many organizations want to use a collection agency *before* turning to an attorney. This is fine, but set a time limit on how long the agency is allowed to retain the account before shifting it to an attorney. In too many cases, accounts languish at a collection agency for far too long, reducing the chances of collection through subsequent litigation.

There may be cases where it makes more sense to bypass a collection agency and go straight to an attorney. For example, if there is a signed document from the customer supporting a claim, the odds of success in court will be much higher, and so may be worth pursuing at once. This scenario arises when there is a promissory note, personal guarantee, or written acknowledgment of a debt. Conversely, when there is a valid dispute over an amount due that makes a favorable outcome in court less likely, it may make more sense to first route the account through a collection agency.

To ensure that accounts are referred to an attorney as expeditiously as possible, set up a weekly status review of all receivables that are above a certain threshold dollar amount, and review them to see if litigation is now the best option for obtaining payment.

Litigation Prescreening

Pursuing litigation against a customer for an unpaid debt is both prolonged and expensive, and has an uncertain outcome. For these reasons, it is not a cost-effective option for most smaller receivables (with the possible exception of a small claims court filing, as noted in a later section). Litigation may not be a valid option even for larger receivables, since a customer may be in such deep financial trouble that it has few unencumbered assets that can be liquidated to pay the creditor.

For these reasons, it is eminently worthwhile to prescreen customers for possible litigation. Any of the following scenarios are ones for which litigation may not be cost-effective:

- There is sufficient uncertainty about the claim that the creditor may not win in court
- The litigation process is inordinately expensive
- The customer has a reputation for fighting litigation for as long as possible
- The customer is known to have few assets and/or large amounts of debt
- Tax liens or other judgments have already been filed against the customer
- There is existing litigation already pending against the customer
- There is a substantial cost associated with seizing, storing, and selling the assets of the customer
- The customer's assets will not fetch much money at auction

However righteous the collections manager may feel about pursuing a claim, doing so simply may not make sense if any of the preceding factors are present. Instead, it may be best to write off the debt and turn the creditor's attention to collecting other receivables. However, the following example presents an alternative scenario that may be worth pursuing.

EXAMPLE

Sharpton Associates is owed $80,000 by Grouch Electronics. Upon further investigation, Sharpton's attorney finds that a bank already has a security interest on all Grouch assets. The bank's loan to Grouch has an outstanding balance of $600,000, and the current balance of Grouch assets is $670,000, leaving $70,000 to be seized if Sharpton decides to pursue the matter in court.

In the preceding example, the bank has over-secured its loan to the debtor, and so would have a significant surplus on hand if it were to foreclose on the loan. In this case, additional assets would still be available to the creditor, were it to pursue the matter further.

Debt Referral to an Attorney

Most creditors maintain an in-house collection function, since doing is less expensive than referring debts to a third party for collection. However, if the in-house collection efforts fail, then the next step is to either refer the matter to a collection agency or to go directly to an attorney. Attorneys can be quite effective in collecting funds, since they represent the next step in the collection process – a lawsuit.

One should consider the fee structure when dealing with an attorney to collect a debt. The attorney may be able to charge the collection fee to the debtor – this works when the original lending or credit agreement states that the debtor agrees to pay all reasonable attorney's fees if the debt is referred to the attorney for collection. Payment will be due to the attorney even if the debtor eventually sends its payment directly to the creditor, rather than the attorney.

Debtor payments are normally made straight to the attorney, who then deposits the payments in an escrow account. The attorney then has a fiduciary duty to safeguard these funds until they can be forwarded to the creditor. The creditor should have an agreement with the attorney regarding the maximum number of days that the attorney can hold onto funds before forwarding them to the creditor.

Matters Relating to the Initiation of a Lawsuit

We touch upon several legal concepts pertaining to the initiation of a lawsuit in the following sub-sections.

Standing to Sue

Plaintiffs cannot bring a lawsuit unless they have *standing to sue*. This means that a plaintiff has a stake in the outcome of a lawsuit.

Long-Arm Statute

It is generally possible for a state court to obtain jurisdiction in a civil lawsuit over a party located outside of the state, under the terms of its long-arm statute. This statute expands a state's jurisdiction to encompass nonresidents, though only if the party has had some minimum threshold level of contact with the state. Thus, someone who entered into a contract in the state or transacted business in the state that caused injury to another party would be accessible under the long-arm statute.

Venue

A lawsuit should be heard in the court of the applicable court system that is closest to where the underlying incident occurred, as well as where evidence and witnesses are available.

The parties to a contract may build into it which court will have jurisdiction to hear a legal dispute between the parties. The forum selected will usually be driven by the dominant party to the contract, which will usually demand that the court stated in the contract be the one closest to its headquarters. This clause is intended to reduce legal costs for that party, and imposes travel costs on the other party, which may have to travel long distances to reach the court stated in the contract.

Naming the Defendant

When filing suit against another party, it is essential to ensure that the defendant be properly named. If a suit were to be filed against a defendant using the incorrect name, then the plaintiff will be unable to access the defendant's assets. Given the severity of the consequences, it is essential to spend extra time verifying the proper name. When filing suit against an individual, it can be useful to include the defendant's middle name, in order to differentiate this person from other people with the same first and last name.

When suing a person who is operating a sole proprietorship, suit should be filed against the name of the defendant, not the name of the business that he or she is operating. This is because the business is nothing more than a trade name; it has no legal standing as a separate entity.

A corporation should be sued under its proper corporate name. This can be found by checking the website of the applicable secretary of state for the correct spelling of the entity.

> **Tip:** Be very clear on your credit application form that the applicant is to provide the complete spelling of their name, as well as the names and addresses of all principals. Also, compare the business name stated on one of their check payments to the name on the credit application, since the name on the check is more likely to be the actual name of the business.

The Lawsuit Process

There are a number of steps involved in the legal proceedings used to collect a debt. The following sequence of events is most commonly followed:

1. *Commencement of the suit.* A collections lawsuit begins with a summons and complaint being filed with the applicable court, along with the payment of a processing fee. In addition, the plaintiff prepares a complaint that summarizes the issues and the damages being sought. Depending on the state, the plaintiff must also sign an affidavit, attesting to the amount owed by the defendant. The summons document is then served upon the defendant by the county sheriff's office, who is thereby notified that an action is being brought by the plaintiff, and the location where the defendant must appear in court. The complaint is attached to the summons. In the case of a corporate defendant, the summons is served on a company officer or its managing agent. In the case of a partnership defendant, the summons is served on one of its partners.

> **Tip:** It is essential to serve the summons to the appropriate party. Otherwise, the defendant can claim that the summons was never received, which can result in the case being dismissed and the plaintiff being forced to start over again.

2. *Administrative actions.* Once the processing fee is paid by the plaintiff, the court issues a case number that uniquely identifies the case.
3. *Defendant response.* The defendant can issue a response to the plaintiff's complaint. This could take the form of a denial of the claims made. Other possibilities are a statement that payment of the debt was already made, or that the obligation is fraudulent. The defendant may also claim that the statute of limitations on payment (which varies by state) has expired, or that the court selected has no jurisdiction over the defendant. In addition, the defendant may elect to issue a counterclaim against the plaintiff, possibly in relation to the plaintiff's claim, or in regard to some other matter. For example, a plumber could sue for services rendered, while the defendant counterclaims for damages caused by the plumber's work.
4. *Response to counterclaim.* If the defendant issues a counterclaim, then the plaintiff can respond to it. Depending on the court, the plaintiff may have to issue a response, or else the defendant can obtain a default judgment.
5. *Arbitration or mediation.* Some courts mandate that arbitration or mediation be used to settle collection cases. In these arrangements, the losing party may

still have the option to seek a trial, though only if this party attended the arbitration or mediation hearings.

6. *Discovery.* During the discovery process, either party can obtain details about the claims or defenses being made by the other party. This can be a prolonged process, but is essential for learning all possible facts about a case. Discovery can employ one or more of the following options:

    a. The defendant submits questions to the plaintiff, asking for details about the complaint being made. For example, the defendant might ask for the calculations associated with a damages claim.

    b. One or more sets of interrogatories (questions) are submitted to the other party, which they are required to answer. Either party can petition the court to not answer certain questions that they feel are not appropriate.

    c. The parties conduct depositions regarding the claims and defenses being made. Any question can be asked that would also be allowed during a trial. A court stenographer records all questions posed and the resulting answers.

    d. Demands are made to the other party to produce documents that are associated with the claim or defense. Either party can petition the court to not produce documents.

Tip: If a court requires that original documents be submitted and those documents were destroyed, then be prepared to testify about the firm's procedures for ensuring that the duplicates provided are accurate. Also, be prepared to discuss the circumstances of the documents' destruction, and why this constitutes common business practice.

---

7. *Motions.* The attorneys for either side may make a variety of motions to the court. For example, a motion could be made to dismiss a complaint, or for summary judgment where sufficient documentary evidence is now available to warrant an immediate decision. A summary judgment motion may be granted when it can be established that there is no credible defense against the evidence. Alternatively, the court may issue a partial summary judgment, in which case the liability of the defendant is established, and the trial is then intended to determine the amount of damages that will be paid. A judge will render a decision on whether each of these motions is granted or denied.

8. *Conference meeting.* Many courts require the opposing parties to meet in a conference to see if the case can be settled. This is done to minimize the amount of court time required for a case.

9. *Trial and judgment.* If the parties cannot settle their differences, then the case will go to trial. A default judgment will result if the defendant does not appear in court, or has not answered the complaint. When judgment is made in favor of the plaintiff, then the county clerk issues a transcript of judgment, stating

the parties involved, the amount of the judgment, the date and location, and the index number.

10. *Search for assets.* After the creditor has obtained a favorable judgment, serve an information subpoena on any third parties who might know where the debtor has assets. Examples of possible targets are relatives, banks, utility companies, landlords, and past and present employers. The intent is to obtain the locations of these assets, so that they can be seized. The creditor can also examine the debtor under oath to ascertain the whereabouts of any assets; in the case of a business, any corporate officers, directors, and employees can also be examined under oath.

11. *Collection.* The transcript of judgment is used as the basis for a lien, which is applied to the real or personal property of the defendant in the county where the judgment was rendered. If the defendant lives in another county, then the plaintiff obtains a certified copy of the judgment from the court and presents it to the relevant court in the county where the debtor now lives. The creditor can then proceed with collection. Another option is for the creditor to garnish the wages of the debtor, which is done by notifying the sheriff's office of the judgment; the sheriff's office then notifies the employer of the debtor. The employer then deducts a portion of the debtor's wages and sends the amount to the sheriff's office, which then forwards it to the creditor. A garnishment can also be served on a bank that maintains a bank account for the debtor; upon receipt, the bank is obligated to transfer the amount stated on the garnishment to the creditor. A final variation is to issue a garnishment to any parties that owe money to the debtor; these parties are then required to make their payments directly to the creditor, rather than to the debtor. For example, if a debtor is a landlord, then its tenants could be required to send their rent payments to the creditor.

Rather than going after the cash reserves of a debtor, a creditor can send a property execution to the sheriff's office. The sheriff then identifies and seizes the indicated property, sells it at public auction, and remits the proceeds to the creditor.[5] The creditor will have to pay for all fees to hold the sale, including advertising the sale and conducting the auction. The sheriff's office will withhold a service fee prior to forwarding the proceeds. Also, the debtor will likely need to be notified in advance and given the option of paying the judgment before the property is seized. There are a variety of local laws that must be observed before real property can be seized and sold.

When a sufficient amount of cash cannot be raised from the seizure of debtor assets and yet the debtor still appears to be enjoying an expensive lifestyle, the creditor can request that the court compel the debtor to make monthly payments to the creditor. If the debtor does not fulfill the terms of this payment, then the debtor can be held in contempt of court.

---

[5] If the seized assets are being used as collateral on a loan, then the sheriff must announce at the auction that the assets are subject to a lien, which must be paid off before the purchaser acquires unencumbered title to the assets.

Some states will vacate default judgments in other states. If a defendant owns assets in one of these states, the plaintiff should sue the debtor within that state on the underlying debt, rather than merely trying to enforce the default judgment.

Settlement Negotiations

The attorney representing each side in a collection suit should be willing to negotiate a settlement throughout the lawsuit process. This can begin as soon as the plaintiff has filed suit, since this is the point at which the debtor will either have to spend significant funds in defense, or pay the demanded amount. Another good time is during or immediately after the discovery process, since this is the point at which any weaknesses in either party's side of the dispute will be revealed. Both sides should be willing to settle for some amount, since the outcome of any trial can vary; witnesses may not appear, technical errors can impact decisions, and the attorneys may make mistakes in how they approach a case. And, the duration of all possible legal proceedings and their associated costs can be immense. In short, a negotiated settlement should always be an option, if only to reduce costs and the uncertainty of the outcome.

If the parties mutually agree to a settlement, then a settlement document must be prepared. This document should contain the following information:

- The identities of the parties and their locations
- The case number
- The terms of the settlement, including payment instructions and the mandated due date
- Whether any attorneys' fees or interest costs are included in the settlement
- A statement that the settlement is voided if payment is not received by a specific date

Arbitration

The plaintiff and defendant may agree to settle their differences through arbitration. This is a private process in which the parties agree to have an independent arbitrator make a decision about the dispute after receiving evidence and hearing arguments. Anywhere from one to three arbitrators are typically used, which are selected from a list provided by the arbitration board in the state where the parties are located.

This process is similar to a trial in that the parties make opening statements and present evidence to the arbitrator. However, the process tends to be less formal and requires less time to complete. In particular, the discovery process is severely reduced, which reduces the legal costs associated with the dispute. Also, the rules of evidence may not be adhered to, so that the arbitrator will peruse all evidence offered.

The arbitrator issues an award after the hearing has been completed. This award may be either binding or non-binding. When arbitration is binding, the decision is considered to be final, and it can be enforced by a court. It is quite difficult to appeal this decision, except in cases where there is a conflict of interest or the arbitrator acted improperly. The winning party should file an application to have the award confirmed by a court within one year of the award date, or else it will be unenforceable.

When arbitration is non-binding, the award is only advisory, and so can be final only if both parties accept it.

Many contracts contain boilerplate clauses requiring the parties to submit their differences to arbitration, on the grounds that this approach is both less expensive and less time-consuming than taking a case to trial.

Small Claims Court

The least expensive form of litigation is through small claims court. This court is designed to handle small-dollar claims on an accelerated basis, with trials typically lasting only a few minutes. In essence, the plaintiff needs to prove that there was an agreement to deliver goods or services, that the delivery was made, and that the defendant defaulted on payment. If there are witnesses, they must appear in court to give testimony. If properly documented, the odds of success are high.

Depending on local requirements, it is usually necessary to file the claim in a court in the county in which the customer resides. Many small claims courts maintain websites, from which complaint forms can be downloaded.

A key issue when using a small claims court is the maximum amount of any awards that the court will grant. If the amount you are seeking to collect is higher, either turn to more traditional litigation, or write off the amount of the debt that is in excess of the maximum court award, and just pursue payment of the maximum allowable amount. The amount of the write-off should be stated on the complaint form sent to the court.

There are a few administrative issues to deal with when using a small claims court. Consider the following:

- *Legal name.* Purchase a credit report on the customer to ensure that you are entering the correct legal name of the customer on the complaint form.
- *Attorney.* Hire a local attorney to represent the company in court. The fee paid could be a combination of a flat fee and a percentage of any proceeds. Since claims must be filed where customers reside, the creditor may have to create a pool of local attorneys from which to draw.

Tip: If a small claims court prohibits attorneys, someone from the creditor must attend the court in person. If so, the cost to travel to a distant court may make this option a less effective one.

Small claims court is an excellent way to obtain a low-cost judgment against a debtor, and within a short period of time. The relatively small value of awards granted makes this the obvious litigation path to pursue for the large number of smaller invoice amounts that creditors may have.

Tip: To save money, wait until just before the trial date to see if the defendant wants to settle the case, and *then* hire an attorney to represent you in court.

Money Judgment Collection Tactics

If the creditor obtains a favorable judgment in court, it still faces the task of obtaining payment from the debtor. The court is not responsible for obtaining payment from the debtor – the creditor must do so.

Obtaining payment may require seizing debtor assets in payment of the debt, so the first task is to determine where the assets are located. One option is to conduct a judgment debtor examination, where the debtor is asked under oath about the locations and amounts of all assets. Debtors must appear in court for this examination, or else the court will issue a warrant for their arrest.

Once the creditor knows where personal property assets are located, it can contact the sheriff having jurisdiction over the county in which the assets are located, and request that they be seized and sold at a public auction.

Tip: When seizing assets, be aware that other entities may have senior claims on those assets. A lien search will uncover these claims.

In some cases, and especially in family-run businesses, the debtor may attempt to shift its assets away from the corporate shell, where they are more difficult to locate. If you suspect that this is a possibility, ask the court to issue a restraining notice to the debtor, prohibiting it from disposing of any assets. An asset restraining order is particularly effective when it targets a debtor's bank accounts. Unfortunately, an asset restraining order can only be requested after the creditor has obtained a favorable judgment against a debtor. It may have taken many months of effort to obtain the judgment, so the debtor will have had that entire period in which to move assets. Consequently, there may be few assets to which the restraining order can be applied.

If a not sufficient amount of funds has been raised through the seizure of personal property, another option is to place a lien on the real property of the debtor, which can be accomplished with a notice of judgment filing through the secretary of state. *Real property* is defined as land and any property attached to the land (such as buildings). This approach does not result in immediate payment, but makes it more difficult for the debtor to sell its assets to third parties, since clear title cannot be transferred until the lien is settled. It may be possible to request a judicial foreclosure of the property, in which case the creditor can be paid from the proceeds of the asset sale (assuming there are no senior liens on the property that must be settled first).

Tip: A money judgment continues to accumulate interest at the legal rate of interest mandated by the state government, so be sure to add it to the amount of the judgment when collecting payment.

Never agree to set aside a money judgment in favor of an agreement by the debtor to pay under a promissory note. The debtor should have agreed to this before the creditor pursued litigation. The only reason a debtor wants to introduce the possibility of a promissory note is to have the judgment set aside, after which payment can be prolonged yet again.

In cases where the creditor is pursuing payment from an individual, it can apply to the court to issue a garnishment. A garnishment requires the employer of an individual to withhold a portion of the person's wages and remit them to the creditor. Wage garnishments may yield little cash if the creditor has a low priority after other garnishment claims on the person's wages, such as for child support payments and tax liens. A garnishment can also be repeatedly applied to the bank account of a debtor, which can be used to extract any funds that have been deposited into the account.

Finally, be sure to keep track of the original money judgment, any allowable fees or interest charges that can be legally added to the judgment, and any subtractions for payments made by the debtor. This is useful not only for dealing with the debtor, but also for responding to any inquiries from the court regarding the status of the judgment. Once the full amount of the judgment has been collected, file a *satisfaction of judgment* notice with the court, which closes the case. It may also be necessary to release any garnishments and property liens that are still outstanding.

Property Lien Strategy

A common collection strategy is to have a judgment recorded as a lien against property owned by the debtor. If the debtor ever wants to sell the property (which may be years later), the buyer of the property will demand that the debtor pay off the debt associated with the lien, on the grounds that the buyer does not want to take on property that is burdened by a lien.

It may not always seem worthwhile to place a lien on a debtor's property, especially when the debtor may not have an interest in selling the property for years. However, this can be a valuable strategy in times when interest rates are declining. If the debtor wants to refinance a mortgage at a lower interest rate, it will be necessary to clear all liens first, which will require the debtor to pay off the associated debts. In this situation, it may be very much in the interests of the debtor to do so, since the lower cost of interest associated with a refinancing could more than offset the cost to eliminate the liens.

Dealing with a Fraudulent Conveyance

When a judgment is made against a debtor, the debtor might try to hide assets through a variety of fraudulent conveyances. For example, someone might shift assets to his children's bank accounts or transfer his interest in the family home to his spouse. If these transfers can be proven to be fraudulent transfers of property, then they can be accessed by a creditor. A creditor will be able to make a fair case that an asset transfer was fraudulent by proving that it was made without fair consideration, or if the transfer renders the debtor insolvent. A good way to make this case is to conduct a title search in the county where the debtor is located, to determine who received the person's property and how much was paid for it.

Tip: Any attempt at setting aside a fraudulent conveyance must be initiated before the statute of limitations expires, so be clear about the available time frame for investigating these conveyances.

Summary

It cannot be overemphasized just how long and expensive it is to pursue the lawsuit option. The number of steps we described in this chapter for the conduct of a lawsuit should make that clear. Consequently, it always makes sense to make inquiries of the opposing party's counsel at various points in the lawsuit process to see if a settlement can be achieved that is reasonable for both parties.

Chapter 6
Dealing with a Debtor Bankruptcy

Introduction

A debtor may become so overwhelmed with debt that there is no reasonable prospect of paying it off. When this is the case, bankruptcy laws can be used to mitigate or even eliminate debts, allowing the bankrupt party a fresh start. In this chapter, we cover the bankruptcy process for both individuals and businesses. This information can be quite useful from a collections perspective, to understand the options for being paid when a debtor enters bankruptcy.

Types of Bankruptcy

When a business enters bankruptcy protection, it may choose to proceed under either Chapter 7 or Chapter 11 of the bankruptcy code. The essential differences between the two are as follows:

- *Chapter 7.* The intent is to liquidate the business, so operations are halted and assets are sold off. This is a good solution when a business is experiencing increased competition, declining sales and recurring losses, so it is time to shut down the firm in an orderly manner, to keep its assets from being frittered away in a vain attempt to support the business. Secured creditors recover the amounts owed to them out of their collateral, while unsecured creditors are paid on a pro rata basis. In the unlikely event that there is some residual cash, it is paid out to shareholders.
- *Chapter 11.* The intent is to reorganize the debtor, which is done through negotiations with creditors to revise the capital structure and operations of the business in order to return it to profitability. The management team is usually retained in Chapter 11, and is responsible for proposing a reorganization plan within six months.[6] If a majority of the creditors vote in favor of this plan, then the court will confirm it, and the plan will be binding on all creditors.

It is possible for a Chapter 11 filing to be converted into a Chapter 7 filing. This is most likely when an initial attempt to resuscitate a debtor fails, leaving liquidation as the best remaining option.

---

[6] Which can be extended by the court for an additional 14 months.

EXAMPLE

Hedgehog Manufacturing is experiencing financial difficulties. If liquidated, it will yield $10 million of cash for the payment of its creditors, who are owed $15 million. However, its value as a going concern is $25 million, which is calculated as the present value of its projected cash flows if it were to remain in business. Under this latter scenario, Hedgehog offers to convert the $15 million of liabilities into shares in the company, valued at $15 million. Thus, the creditors can pursue the Chapter 7 option and take a guaranteed $5 million loss, or take a chance on ownership of the company by avoiding a loss entirely and hoping to sell their shares at a later date.

Because management can stay in place during a Chapter 11 proceeding, organizations in significant financial trouble have a tendency to begin with a Chapter 11 filing in order to stay in control of the proceedings, and then liquidate the business.

Chapter 13 is a bankruptcy proceeding in which an individual can reorganize his or her personal finances, using a process overseen by the courts. Individuals are required to submit a plan for repaying creditors within three to five years, where the creditors receive a significant proportion of the funds they have loaned out. This approach works best when a person has a sufficient amount of ongoing income to repay creditors. Alternatively, an individual can use the Chapter 7 process described earlier to have all or a large part of his or her debts discharged; this only happens after one's liquid assets have been used to repay some of the outstanding debts.

Bankruptcy Players (Business)

A bankruptcy may involve two parties that are not found in most other business transactions – the trustee and the creditors' committee. These key players are described in the following sub-sections.

The Trustee

A trustee may be appointed to manage the affairs of a bankruptcy estate, usually one that is scheduled to be liquidated under Chapter 7 of the Code. This is a substantial role, for the trustee is responsible for the following tasks:

- Assemble all property owned by the estate and render an accounting for it.
- Identify and collect all assets related to sham sales, fraudulent transfers, and voidable preferences.
- Convert all property to cash, taking a sufficient amount of time to obtain fair prices.
- Review proofs of claim to determine if they are allowable, objecting to claims that cannot be proven.
- File reports with the bankruptcy court as needed.
- File final tax reports with the applicable government entities.
- Recommend whether to discharge the debtor following the conclusion of bankruptcy proceedings.

If the trustee is called upon to manage the affairs of a debtor in Chapter 11, then add to the preceding responsibilities all additional tasks normally taken on by management.

The Creditors' Committee

The creditors' committee is comprised of representatives of the debtor's unsecured creditors, usually from those creditors with the seven largest unsecured claims. This committee represents the following creditors, acting on their behalf as a bargaining agent with the debtor:

- Bondholders
- Contingent claim holders
- Holders of the unsecured portion of secured debt
- Trade creditors

The committee is active throughout the bankruptcy period, being engaged in the following tasks:

- Determining whether the debtor should remain in operation or be liquidated
- Discussing and negotiating over the debtor's formulation of a plan
- Discussing the administration of the case with the debtor or trustee
- Investigating the debtor's financial affairs

If the debtor cannot formulate a viable plan by the end of the period allowed it by the court, the committee can propose an alternative plan.

In order to maintain a detailed level of oversight, the committee may hire outside experts to assist it, such as accountants, attorneys, and investment bankers. With their assistance, the committee may find that the asset base of the debtor is declining, and so will be more active in pushing for immediate liquidation of the business in order to preserve their shares of its residual assets. The committee may also request that a key performance indicators report be issued to it at regular intervals, so that committee members can evaluate the financial condition of the debtor throughout the bankruptcy process.

EXAMPLE

Garuda Mining has entered Chapter 11 bankruptcy protection, so a creditors' committee has been formed. The committee suspects that Garuda is maintaining a number of coal delivery contracts that are deeply unprofitable, so it hires a local law firm to investigate these contracts. The investigation reveals that half of Garuda's coal delivery contracts are losing money, so the committee recommends to the court that these contracts be terminated, and that a trustee be brought in to take over the business.

> **Tip:** Generally, the creditors' committee should play a more active role when a debtor is relatively small, since the firm is more likely to have minimal controls over its assets, which may therefore decline rapidly in value as they are dissipated.

There is usually only one creditors' committee, though additional committees may be formed to represent any parties with special interests. For example, a separate committee may be assembled when the debtor is subject to substantial numbers of asbestos exposure claims.

The Involuntary Bankruptcy Petition

A debtor may have no choice in whether to file for bankruptcy, due to an involuntary bankruptcy petition being filed by creditors. This is a petition that a debtor be sent into bankruptcy proceedings. This situation usually arises when a debtor is very late in paying bills to a number of creditors, who feel that they are more likely to be paid if the business is forced into bankruptcy. This process is time-consuming and expensive, so it is usually followed only if creditors believe they are at considerable risk of not being paid via any other action, and the debtor is holding assets that can be used to pay its debts.

Several conditions must be met before creditors can file for an involuntary bankruptcy. Depending on the situation, a minimum of three creditors must force the issue, and only if a certain unpaid debt level has been reached for the qualifying claims. Further, the debtor must generally not be paying its debts as they come due for payment.

An involuntary bankruptcy petition is served to the debtor, along with a summons. The debtor can consent to the petition or elect to fight it in court. If the court decides in favor of the creditors, an order for relief is entered and the debtor is placed in bankruptcy proceedings. If the court decides in favor of the debtor, the creditors may be liable for the debtor's court costs.

An involuntary bankruptcy petition is more likely to result in the liquidation of the debtor, since the debtor has no warning, and so is not in a position to stockpile cash prior to the bankruptcy filing.

The Bankruptcy Process (Business)

When management wants to enter bankruptcy protection, the first step is to file Form 201, the *Voluntary Petition for Non-Individuals Filing for Bankruptcy*. This form identifies the debtor and its type of business, provides estimates of available funds, the number of creditors, estimated assets and liabilities, and the chapter of the Code under which the debtor is filing.

When a business enters bankruptcy, this triggers an *automatic stay*, which requires creditors (even secured ones) to stop any debt collection activities, thereby preventing them from seizing assets, while the debtor's obligation to pay interest is suspended. Instead, all company assets are now owned by the bankruptcy estate, which operates under the jurisdiction of the bankruptcy court. The court may appoint a trustee to manage the estate and all aspects of the related bankruptcy case, or it may allow current managers to do so in the case of a Chapter 11 filing (known as *debtor-in-possession*). A debtor-in-possession has the same powers as a trustee. The court can appoint a trustee to replace the debtor-in-possession; this is done when the court believes that the appointment of a trustee will be in the best interests of the creditors.

If a Chapter 7 filing has been made, then an interim trustee is appointed shortly after the petition is filed; this person is usually confirmed as the permanent trustee at a later hearing, unless the creditors elect a different trustee. There is no debtor-in-possession for a Chapter 7 filing – only an appointed trustee.

Creditors send proofs of claim to the trustee or debtor-in-possession regarding the amounts owed to them, while a shareholder files a proof of interest. Doing so is intended to notify the trustee or debtor-in-possession that a claim exists, and the amount of that claim. These documents are not needed if the debtor has already listed the amounts owed to these parties in its schedule of liabilities.

When a proof of claim is filed, it is assumed to be valid unless the debtor or another creditor challenges it. Claims may be disallowed in certain highly specific cases, such as for claims by the debtor's attorney when they exceed the reasonable value of the services provided to the debtor.

Creditors and equity holders are then separated into classes, where the classes are based on common characteristics[7]. Examples of these classes are:

- Each secured creditor with distinct collateral
- Secured creditors with shared collateral
- Unsecured creditors
- Holders of common stock
- Holders of preferred stock

The debtor-in-possession has 120 days from the bankruptcy petition date to propose a plan to the court, as well as another 60 days to convince creditors and shareholders to accept the plan. The court is allowed to extend these deadlines by as much as 14 months, thereby giving the debtor-in-possession a great deal of control over the process.

Once a bankruptcy plan has been formulated, it must be accepted by every class of creditors whose claims would be impaired by the plan, as well as by every class of shareholders whose ownership interests would be impaired. The voting rule that applies to approval of a bankruptcy plan is:

- Each class accepts a plan when a majority of the members of that class vote in favor of it; and
- Those members voting in favor comprise at least 2/3 of the total value of the claims or interests associated with that class.

---

[7] The members of a class should be grouped based on the similarity of their claims, not the similarity of the creditors.

If all classes accept the plan, then the plan is officially confirmed. If a class does not accept a proffered bankruptcy plan, the judge can still confirm the plan, as long as the plan is fair and equitable toward that class. If the plan is not accepted by the end of the period during which the debtor has the exclusive right to file a plan, then the court must consider plans submitted by other parties.

Note: There may be a challenge to a creditor's or shareholder's right to vote for a bankruptcy plan. If the court finds that a vote was cast in bad faith, then it can exclude that vote from the voting tabulation. For example, when a party with a conflict of interest casts a vote, the judge can elect to disregard the vote. If that party was the sole member of a class of creditors or shareholders, the exclusion means that the party's class is deemed to have accepted the bankruptcy plan.

Note: There is no exclusivity period for filing a plan if a trustee is appointed by the court, so creditors wanting to submit a plan for consideration right away may therefore petition the court to appoint a trustee in the early days of a bankruptcy.

A bankruptcy plan must include the following topics:
- State the classes of creditor claims and shareholder interests.
- Specify any class of claims or interests that is not impaired under the plan.
- Specify the treatment of any class of claims or interests that is impaired under the plan.
- Provide the same treatment for each claim or interest within a particular class, unless a holder of a claim or interest agrees to less favorable treatment.
- Provide adequate means for implementation, such as the debtor retaining most of the property of the estate, merging the debtor with another entity, sale or distribution of the property, satisfaction or modification of liens, curing or waiving defaults, extending debt maturity dates, altering debt interest rates, the issuance of securities of the debtor, and so forth.
- Provide for the inclusion in the debtor's charter a provision prohibiting the issuance of nonvoting equity securities, and providing an appropriate distribution of power among the various voting classes of securities.
- Contain only provisions that are consistent with the interests of creditors and shareholders in regard to the selection of officers, directors, and trustees under the plan.

In addition, the plan may include the following components:
- Either impair or leave unimpaired any class of claims or interests.
- Provide for the assumption, rejection, or assignment of any executory contract or unexpired lease not previously rejected.

- Provide for the settlement or adjustment of any claim or interest belonging to the debtor.
- Provide for the sale of the property of the estate and the distribution of any proceeds to the holders of claims or interests.

The plan represents a balancing act between the requirements of the creditors and the debtor, where the creditors want to be paid a higher proportion of their claims up front and in cash, while the debtor wants to reserve as much cash as possible and reduce its debt load, to facilitate its recovery. Creditors will also likely want to retain as much of the debt owed to them as possible, while the debtor will want to convert a significant proportion of it into equity, thereby creating a more conservative and sustainable financial structure for its future operations.

The court will not approve the plan unless all priority claims have been provided for, such as administrative expenses.

If the determination is made to liquidate the debtor, the trustee will be responsible for auctioning off its assets in a well-organized manner that is intended to maximize the amount of funds received. Once funds have been received, the Code provides that they should be distributed in the following manner:

1. To the holders of priority claims
2. To the holders of general unsecured claims who filed a proof of claim
3. To the holders of general unsecured claims who filed late
4. Payments for fines, penalties, forfeitures, or damages suffered by claim holders
5. Interest due on the preceding claims at the legal rate, accrued from the date when the bankruptcy petition was filed
6. Any remaining balance to the debtor

If a debt is not repaid in some way within the reorganization plan, then the debt is cancelled when the court rules that the bankruptcy case is complete.

When the intent is to liquidate assets and the preceding tasks have been completed, the trustee makes a final report to the court, and is discharged from any further responsibilities related to the case. These same tasks can be conducted under a Chapter 11 filing, with either the debtor-in-possession or a trustee in charge of the liquidation of assets.

The process is different when the debtor intends to emerge from bankruptcy as a functioning business. Once the plan has been approved and implemented, the debtor receives a discharge of all debts that are not dealt with in the plan. This also means that any taxes not provided for in the plan will be discharged once the plan implementation has been completed.

EXAMPLE

Absolution Corporation (maker of church paraphernalia) has incurred a $1,000 occupational privilege tax liability. This is not considered a priority claim, so it is classified as an unsecured claim. The firm's plan states that unsecured creditors will receive 32% of their claims. As a result, $320 of the claim is paid out, while the remaining $680 of the tax is discharged.

Chapter 7 and Chapter 13 Bankruptcy (Individual)

An individual who is contemplating bankruptcy protection can use either Chapter 7 or Chapter 13 of the federal bankruptcy law to do so. When Chapter 7 is used, the person can retain a modest amount of assets (known as exempt assets), while all other assets are sold off to raise cash, which is then used to pay the claims of creditors. Any creditor claims not paid off through this process are discharged. Further, current creditors have no claim on the person's future income.

EXAMPLE

Paul is overwhelmed with debt, and so files for Chapter 7 bankruptcy protection. At the time of the filing, he has unsecured debt of $240,000. He gets to retain a small number of exempt assets, leaving $30,000 of nonexempt assets, all of which are sold and converted into cash. This cash is distributed to Paul's creditors on a pro rata basis, so that each one receives $1 for every $8 owed. The creditors must write off the remaining $210,000 that they are owed.

A person who wants to use Chapter 7 for bankruptcy protection must pass two tests; if he or she cannot do so, then only Chapter 13 bankruptcy protection is available. The first of these tests is the median income test, under which the person's family income must be equal to or less than the median income of their state of residence. If a person passes this test, then Chapter 7 protection can be used. If the person's income is too high to pass this test, then the means test is also applied. Under the means test, expenses representing typical family expenses (as determined by the government) are subtracted from the person's actual income. If the resulting disposal income is judged to be insufficient to pay off his or her prepetition debts from postpetition income, then the person will qualify for Chapter 7 protection. When an individual fails these tests, the only remaining option is Chapter 13 protection.

A creditor can claim that an individual's debt should not be discharged in Chapter 7 proceedings. There are several valid reasons for doing so, including the person making false claims about his or her personal finances when requesting a credit extension, concealing the property of the estate in the year prior to when the bankruptcy petition was filed, and falsifying one's financial records. Further, if a person obtains a discharge of debts through fraudulent misrepresentations or fraud, the court may revoke the discharge within the following year.

In Chapter 7 proceedings, the claims of secured creditors have absolute priority over those of unsecured creditors. This means that secured creditors are paid first, after which any residual cash is paid out to the unsecured creditors. However, there are some permutations on the general concept. First, the collateral that a creditor claims may be worth more than the amount of the underlying claim. When this is the case, the asset is sold, the secured creditor is paid, and any residual cash is allocated to the unsecured creditors. Alternatively, the collateral may be worth less than the amount of the underlying claim. When this is the case, the asset is sold, the secured creditor is paid, and its remaining claim is lumped in with those of the other unsecured creditors.

The Chapter 13 bankruptcy process is more oriented toward delaying the payment of debts than of eliminating them, and so is much less favorable for a person who is operating under a significant debt burden. Under Chapter 13, an individual can put forward a debt payment plan that will pay outstanding amounts through a series of installment payments, under the supervision of a bankruptcy court. Creditors prefer this approach, since they are more likely to recover a larger percentage of the receivables due to them; there is also a benefit for the debtor, who can retain a larger proportion of his or her assets than would have been the case under a Chapter 7 filing. In a Chapter 13 filing, there is no specific provision for liquidating assets and transferring the proceeds to creditors.

A creditor cannot file an involuntary Chapter 13 bankruptcy petition for a person. Instead, it can only be filed by a debtor who has sufficient regular income to allow the person to make ongoing debt repayments. Also, a Chapter 13 filing is only allowed when the filer has incurred debts that are primarily *consumer debt*; these debts are owed due to the purchase of goods for individual or household consumption. Examples of consumer debt are credit card debt, student loans, mortgages, and auto loans.

> **Note:** A sole proprietorship can file for Chapter 13 protection.

A key element of an individual's estate in a Chapter 13 filing is his or her future income (which is not included in a Chapter 7 filing). The inclusion of future income makes it easier for creditors to receive payments from the person's future income.

When a debtor files a Chapter 13 payment plan, this must also include information about the person's financial situation, as well as a budget of income and expenses through the plan period (which may cover a three to five-year period). The payment plan must be approved by secured and unsecured creditors, though the court can override a negative vote from a secured creditor if the plan provides for full payment. When there are objections from unsecured creditors, the court may override these votes if the individual will commit all of his or her disposable income to pay these parties. If the plan is confirmed, the person then makes consolidated monthly payments to the plan trustee, who in turn is responsible for passing these payments along to the creditors.

Once all payments required under the plan have been remitted, the court discharges all remaining unpaid unsecured debt. However, the person will continue to be responsible for any unpaid taxes, which are not covered by the discharge.

The Bankruptcy Process (Individual)

When an individual files for bankruptcy protection, the first step is to obtain prepetition counseling. This is a discussion with a representative of a non-profit credit counseling service about the types and uses of credit, as well as personal budgeting.

When filing a voluntary bankruptcy petition, an individual must provide the bankruptcy court with a list of secured and unsecured creditors, a list of all property owned by the person, and a statement of his or her financial affairs, as well as monthly income and expenses. Employer pay stubs must also be provided for the past 60 days, as well as a copy of the person's federal income tax return for the preceding year. Finally, one must also provide a certificate, stating that prepetition counseling has been completed. If an attorney is representing the individual, then the attorney must certify that the information provided is correct.

Once the bankruptcy petition has been filed for a person who is filing for the first time, the court puts an *automatic stay* in place. This stay prohibits nearly all creditors from continuing their collection activities. This means that creditors cannot call, collect money, foreclose on one's home, repossess a car, or place a lien on one's property. However, creditors can go to court to ask the judge to lift the automatic stay.

Note: An automatic stay does not apply to domestic support obligations, such as child support and alimony payments.

The next step is for the person to attend a meeting of creditors, which is conducted by the bankruptcy trustee. The trustee will verify one's identity and ask questions about the petition and one's finances, such as the nature of any property dispositions prior to the bankruptcy filing. Creditors can, but usually do not, attend in order to ask questions. The trustee is now the legal representative of the person's estate, and as such has the power to sell the individual's property.

Each creditor can file a proof of claim, on which is stated the amount of a claim against the person. When a creditor's claim is secured but the amount claimed exceeds the value of the associated collateral, the creditor can also become an unsecured claimant for the remaining amount.

An individual must also receive postpetition counseling in the responsible use of credit, as well as in how to adhere to a personal financial plan.

The next step is for the court to issue a bankruptcy discharge, which stops the automatic stay. This discharge will identify which types of debt the person still owes, such as student loan debt and recent tax obligations. By default, all other debts are cancelled. Creditors may continue to pursue the person for any remaining debts.

In rare cases, a person might enter into a reaffirmation agreement, under which he or she agrees to pay a debt that will be discharged in bankruptcy. This agreement must be entered into and filed with the court before it grants a discharge of debts. Court approval must be obtained if this agreement will cause undue hardship for the bankrupt person or family members.

The Bankruptcy Estate (Individual)

Once a bankruptcy case has begun, a bankruptcy estate is created. Contained within this estate is all of a debtor's property interests in existence as of the date when the bankruptcy petition was filed. Certain additional items are included in this estate, such as any life insurance proceeds, inheritances, property from divorce settlements, and gifts that are to be received within 180 days of the filing date of the petition. Furthermore, any earnings from the estate assets, such as interest income and rent, are part of the estate. Also included in the estate is any fraudulent transfer of property that the debtor made during the two years prior to the bankruptcy filing. A transfer is considered to be fraudulent if it was made with the intent to hinder a creditor, or the debtor received less than a reasonable value equivalent from the transfer.

EXAMPLE

Justin owes several million dollars to a group of unsecured creditors. He files for Chapter 7 bankruptcy protection on April 1. On the preceding January 12, he sold a Tesla Roadster worth $120,000 to a friend, Jonathan, for $80,000. Jonathan is a bona fide purchaser who has no clue that Justin is in financial difficulty. The bankruptcy court can void the sale of the Tesla as a fraudulent transfer, because it transpired within two years of the bankruptcy filing date, and because Justin received less than a reasonable value equivalent. However, since Jonathan is a bona fide purchaser, the court must pay back the $80,000 purchase price in exchange for the car.

Exempt property is excluded from this estate. Creditors cannot claim exempt property, so the debtor can keep it. The exact amounts of these exclusions are updated by the government every few years; the general types of exempt property include one's ownership interest in a home, one vehicle, household goods, implements, clothes, and tools. In addition, the person can continue to receive social security benefits, welfare payments, veteran's benefits, and disability benefits. A capped amount of retirement funds in a tax-exempt account can also be retained, as well as any alimony, child support, profit sharing, and annuity payments.

A central part of these exemptions is one's ownership interest in a home. The amount that can be retained in bankruptcy is quite small, so if a person's equity in the property exceeds this cap, the trustee is authorized to sell the property in order to access the extra value.

> **Note:** A few states, such as Texas and Florida, have no cap at all on the amount of home equity that a bankrupt person can retain. This has presented the opportunity for heavily leverage people to move to these states and acquire property there in order to shelter from creditors.

Bankruptcy Collection Activities

While it is certainly undesirable for a seller to be caught in a bankruptcy situation, there are a number of actions that can be taken to mitigate the amount of the loss. These actions are:

- *Stop goods in transit.* If there are any goods in transit to the customer that have not yet been delivered, contact the freight carrier and have them return the goods to the seller.
- *Stop orders in process.* If there are any orders from the customer that have not yet been shipped, halt them at once.
- *Terminate credit.* The credit department immediately sets the customer's credit limit to zero, so the system flags any new orders placed as requiring payment in cash.
- *Preference claim defenses.* If the customer has paid the company within the last 90 days, consult with an attorney regarding the seller's defenses against a claim that a preferential transfer was made.
- *Proof of delivery.* Request proof of delivery for all unpaid items from freight carriers, since this information will be needed when filing a claim for payment.
- *File a claim.* Be sure to file a proof of claim form for all amounts owed, and do so promptly, so the claim is recorded with the trustee. The electronic filing of claims is usually possible, in which case the creditor can confirm receipt by reviewing the claims register for the case. If the claim is instead filed manually with the court, obtain a written confirmation of receipt. If any claims are disputed, address the issues aggressively in order to resolve them as soon as possible. Disputes may be in regard to the amount of the claim or its order of priority for payment. Any claims filed after the *bar date* set by the court will be rejected. The bar date is the date by which claims must be received.

> **Tip:** Verify that a proof of claim has been filed for the correct case and in the correct district. The creditor has no recourse if the proof of claim is filed for the wrong case.

- *Report fraudulent conveyances.* If the creditor has a large claim and so stands to recover a significant amount, it may be worthwhile to engage in research to find any customer assets that may have been illegally transferred to a third party. If located, report these assets to the trustee.
- *Pursue third parties.* If the bankrupt entity is a sole proprietorship or a general partnership, pursue the personal assets of the owners of the entity, since there is no corporate protection afforded to the owners of these types of entities. Also, pursue any third party that issued a personal guarantee to pay the debts of the customer. However, be aware that an individual may also claim personal bankruptcy protection in order to eliminate the liability represented by a guarantee.

> **Tip:** Do not send original documents to the court as part of a proof of claim, since they may be lost. Instead, photocopies are a sufficient form of evidence.

In addition, we cover asset reclamation and the sale of a creditor claim later in this section.

> **Tip:** All collection activities against a debtor must cease as soon as the creditor receives notice that the debtor has filed for bankruptcy protection. To ensure that the filing is real, obtain the case number and confirm it with the court.

Asset Reclamation

If a customer declares bankruptcy, it may still be possible to reclaim goods sold to that customer, rather than filing a claim with the bankruptcy court To do so, the following conditions must be present:

- The sale was made on credit
- The customer was already insolvent when it received the goods
- The demand for return of the goods is made within 10 business days of the date when the customer received them
- The customer still has possession of the goods

If all of these conditions can be met, then make the claim in writing, and send the claim via an overnight delivery service that obtains a receipt signature from the customer. This signature provides legal evidence of receipt. An example of the reclamation demand letter appears in the following exhibit.

Sample Reclamation Demand Letter

Debtor Name
Debtor Address

Re: Debtor's case number

Dear [name]:

This letter constitutes a notice of demand for the return of certain goods purchased by the debtor from [creditor name]. Please take notice that pursuant to [state] commercial code [section number], and by virtue of the debtor's insolvency, the seller hereby demands the segregation and return of all the goods currently in your possession and delivered to you on or after [cutoff date] pursuant to the attached list of invoices. Unless you authorize the return of the goods immediately, further additional measures will be taken.

Please contact me immediately to make arrangements to allow the seller to reclaim the goods. Thank you.

If the asset reclamation claim is upheld by the bankruptcy court, the company may be paid back in one of the following ways:

- The goods are returned
- Cash payment of the full claim is made
- The creditor is granted a security interest in the goods

Sell a Creditor Claim

When a customer goes bankrupt, the seller can file a claim with the bankruptcy court to be paid for any related outstanding receivables. Though the seller may eventually receive compensation, it may not be for a long time, and for much less than the billed amount. Alternatively, and possibly worse, the seller may be paid with ownership shares in the customer, which can be quite difficult to liquidate.

To avoid the prolonged process of being paid through a bankruptcy court, it may instead be possible to sell the claim to a third party investor immediately, for cash. The investor takes over responsibility for pursuing the claim, hoping to eventually earn a reasonable return on the initial investment, as paid to the seller. Alternatively, the investor may collect a number of these claims and use them to:

- Gain control over the customer; or
- Block reorganization plans; or
- Resell the combined claims for a higher price to another investor

In order to sell a claim to an investor, the seller must verify with the customer that the claim for payment is not disputed. If so, the investor is much more willing to buy the claim. The investor then estimates the amount of the claim that will eventually be paid, discounts the result for the estimated amount of time that will pass before payment is made, and factors in a profit to arrive at an amount to offer the seller for the claim.

As part of the sale, the seller and investor must agree upon the terms of an *assignment of claim* agreement. The investor then notifies the bankruptcy court of the sale, which forwards the notification to the customer. If the customer has no objection, the bankruptcy court substitutes the name of the investor for the name of the original seller as the owner of the claim.

The seller should be wary of a number of terms on an assignment of claim agreement that are intended to shift the risk of bankruptcy court nonpayment from the investor to the seller. These issues include:

- The seller is required to repurchase the claim from the investor if the claim is not made
- The seller must pay the investor interest charges if the claim is not paid
- The seller must repurchase all claims subsequently disputed
- The investor is allowed to delay payment to the seller

If these terms are excessively onerous, the seller should strongly consider retaining its claim and waiting for a payout from the bankruptcy court, or at least finding a different investor that is willing to pay under more reasonable terms.

Summary

In the case of a business, the bankruptcy process is designed for the benefit of creditors, not the business. Shareholder interests will likely be wiped out, with creditors electing to either be paid from the assets of the firm, accepting shares in it, or some combination of the two. In the case of an individual, the bankruptcy process is designed to give the person a fresh start while still making some provision for creditors. These are entirely different perspectives on how to treat the debtor.

Glossary

A

Agent. An individual or business that acts on behalf of another party.

Arbitration. The use of an arbitrator to settle a dispute.

B

Bankruptcy. A legal proceeding involving a person or business that is unable to repay its outstanding debts.

Bounced check. A check that cannot be processed because the account on which it is drawn contains insufficient funds.

C

Collateral. An asset or group of assets that a borrower has pledged as security for a loan.

Creditor. An entity to which money is owed.

D

Debtor. An entity that owes a sum of money to a third party.

Debtor-in-possession. A party that has filed for Chapter 11 protection, but still holds property to which creditors have a legal claim under a lien or other security interest.

Destination contract. When the seller delivers the goods to the destination specified in the contract, after which title passes to the buyer.

F

Financing statement. A legal form that a creditor files to give notice that it has an interest in the personal property of a debtor.

Firm offer rule. When a merchant issues a written and signed promise to keep an offer open, this creates an irrevocable offer.

G

Goods. Tangible items that can be transported when they are linked to a contract.

L

Lien. A right to keep possession of property belonging to another person until a debt owed by that person is discharged.

M

Merchant. A party that routinely deals in goods of the kind associated with a transaction, or who holds himself out as having the knowledge or skill associated with such goods.

Mixed sales. When there are elements of both goods and services in a sale.

Mortgage. A loan that the borrower uses to purchase or maintain a home or other form of real estate and agrees to pay back over time, typically in a series of regular payments.

P

Personal property. Any assets other than land or buildings.

Plaintiff. A person who brings a case against another in a court of law.

R

Real property. Land and everything permanently attached to it.

S

Sale. The transfer of goods from a seller to a buyer for a price.

Secured lender. A lender that has a security interest in a borrower's property.

Shipment contract. When the seller is required to deliver the goods to a common carrier, which then transports them to the buyer.

T

Trustee. A party given powers of administration over property held in trust, with a legal obligation to administer it solely for the purposes specified.

Index